INSIDE
THE BRITISH
POLICE

A FORCE AT WORK

Basil Blackwell

363.2
HOL.

© Simon Holdaway 1983

First published 1983
First published in paperback 1984
Reprinted 1984

Basil Blackwell Publisher Limited
108 Cowley Road, Oxford OX4 1JF, England

Basil Blackwell Inc.
432 Park Avenue South, Suite 1505
New York, NY 10016, USA

All names and places mentioned in the text have been
changed to ensure anonymity.

British Library Cataloguing in Publication Data

Holdaway, Simon
    Inside the British police.
    1. Police – Great Britain – Social aspects
    I. Title
    363.2′0941   HV8196
ISBN 0-631-13112-4
ISBN 0-631-13833-1

Printed in Great Britain by
Whitstable Litho Ltd, Kent

16 5 89 (A)

Contents

Preface and Acknowledgements

When the research for this book began the police were a subject of passing interest to most sociologists. As I put the finishing touches to my manuscript a cascade of commentary was flowing over the police: some of the policy issues raised in the final chapter may be overtaken by reform. If the Police and Criminal Evidence Bill, which is presently at the parliamentary committee stage, is not drastically amended, many of the problems that I identify may be compounded rather than made available for open and honest discussion and dealt with by policy. Nevertheless, this preface is not an apologia (save that I should acknowledge here that the theoretical discussion in chapter 2 and all the references have been pared to the bone) but an opportunity to make public thanks to the many people who have given me their support and kindness. I would like to mention some of them.

The staff of the Departments of Sociology and Religious Studies at the University of Lancaster set me on my academic path. Michael Banton, Mike Chatterton, Peter Manning, Terence Morris, Maurice Punch and Paul Rock have been particularly helpful during and since the early days of research. My colleagues in the Department of Sociological Studies at the University of Sheffield must have wondered how they would cope with a police sergeant turned sociology lecturer. I am grateful to them for support. Some police officers who have stayed the course better than I and are doing what they can to promote change in the police service have caused me to think hard about the sort of criticism I might make of the police. Next, David Thomas, Geoff Anderson and Lynn Pocock, colleagues in the team ministry of the parish of Gleadless, Sheffield, have frequently refused this 'worker priest' any retreat into ecclesiastical havens – for which I am more than grateful. The Trustees of the Nuffield Foundation kindly awarded me a Social Science Fellowship, which enabled the writing of this text. Chapter 1 appeared originally as 'An inside job: a case study of covert research on the police', in Martin Bulmer (ed.), *Social Research Ethics*, London: Macmillan, 1982; chapter 3 is an adaptation of 'The police station', *Urban Life*, 9 (1), 1980, pp. 79–100. Finally, my family, Hilary, Ruth, Ben, David and Peter, have taken the brunt of the pressure of work and made my survival possible.

Some readers may find this a negative work. It is not intended as such. My hope is for a new police. The script was completed during the season of Lent, which seems appropriate. In that season we try to recognize our human limitations and weakness as integral aspects of our personal growth. The trouble is that we dislike such a searching of ourselves; it is uncomfortable and at times painful, offering no escape from conflict. What is true for us is no less true for institutions like the police. If I desire anything for this book, it is that it may make a small contribution to our search for a more loving and just society and therefore a more loving and just police. It is offered with thanksgiving.

Sheffield   S. H.

1

Researching the Police: Methodology and Constraints

Ten years have passed since this study of policing began. A great deal has changed. I was then a police sergeant who, with about 120 other officers, patrolled Hilton subdivision, an area close to the centre of one of Britain's major cities. Hilton has changed. During my two-year posting there the extensive schemes of redevelopment were obvious to anyone who walked its streets. Rows of terraced houses had been demolished or boarded up to make way for council houses and flats. Barren sites awaiting new houses were skirted by corrugated iron murals, the work of action groups rather than of local residents.

A large population lived in the midst of this redevelopment. If you shopped in, or just wandered along, any of Hilton's main streets, you would hear the dialects of the many black British and immigrant peoples, including those of Cypriot and Irish families. They lived in houses which, frankly, neither you nor I (nor they, if there were an alternative) would choose to inhabit. Two years before my research began in the mid-1970s a social survey of the area identified its housing conditions as the worst in the borough; only about one-fifth of the 53,000 people who lived in Hilton had exclusive access to hot water, a bath and an inside lavatory. In the central area of the subdivision, it was estimated, one family in six was headed by a single parent, and 9 per cent of families had four or more children. So Hilton was one of those inner-city areas that manifested all the signs of social deprivation. It was similar to places in which riots took place during the summer of 1981 and, like those places, formed the 'ground' on which many police officers spent their working lives.

Since my time at Hilton the staff of the police station has changed over and again. Many new policies for law enforcement, community relations, patrol and training have been introduced to its officers; the chief officers of the force have begun to enter public and, at times, national political debate about the nature of policing; important reports like those from the Royal Commission on Criminal Procedure (1981) and Lord Scarman's inquiry (Home Office, 1981) have advocated particular reforms for the police; social scientists have produced a string of publications about British policing. In short, we now seem to know a good deal more about our constabularies than we did before. But I remain sceptical – first, about the amount and type of information available to us and, secondly, about the effects of these changes on the constables and sergeants who work on the streets of Hilton and elsewhere in urban Britain.

At the heart of my argument in this book is the claim that a residual core of beliefs and values, of associated strategies and tactics relevant to policing, remains a principal guide for the day-to-day work of the rank-and-file officer. This core of police work – the 'occupational culture' – is what the officers of Hilton would call common sense. Of course, they do not share this common sense in equal measure, but at Hilton it forms the basic reservoir of knowledge about police work on which variations in individual style and specialisms draw. All the resources of policing – the law, force policy and managerial instructions – are refined and reworked in this crucible (Chatterton, 1975a and b; Holdaway, 1977, 1978, 1980; Manning, 1977; Punch, 1979b).

The questions that inform this study are therefore very straightforward. How do the lower-ranked officers at Hilton understand their work, their role as police officers and the geographical area that they police? On the basis of their understanding, how do they carry out their police work? Straightforward as these questions might seem, they have led me into an extensive minefield. And they have remained unresolved. When the law is invoked by an officer who warns, summonses or arrests a person, when a police community relations policy is put into effect as a constable stops a black youth in the street, when a suspect is questioned in a police detention room, when PC 123 walks down the High Street and looks at the people and places around him, questions are begged about how all the potential resources of law and policy make their impact. If we are to understand that impact, one of the most important sources of information will be the observation of day-to-day policing – it is necessary, as Robert Park put it, to 'get the seat of your pants dirty in real research' (Manning, 1972, p. 213).

I found fortune because I was in a unique position to carry out research; before I studied any sociology and during the course of my undergraduate and graduate work I was a police officer. As this was a situation of considerable advantage and yet difficulty, of great excitement and yet discomfort, some of the dilemmas that I encountered as a participant observer should be described before any substantive account of the policing of Hilton is presented (Holdaway, 1982a).

Researching Hilton

'Getting the seat of your pants dirty in real research' is a hazardous business. My research began after graduation, when I returned from university secondment to my force and to work as a sergeant. During my undergraduate studies I learned to conceptualize what seemed highly questionable police practices as the 'occupational culture' of policing – a term well suited to the seminar but less appropriate in the station office and charge room. Ethical problems are not solved by the theorizing of sociologists; neither is it an easy business to find a fit between theoretical inferences drawn from sociological research and possible policy initiatives. This point may seem blindingly obvious – yet in much sociology a background of utopian simplicity is obscured by theoretical complexity. I am aware that if academic curiosity is a driving force for my research, that curiosity is tempered by some moral concern to weigh police practice and, in the longer term, to change it. The issue is whether ethics are the tail that wags the researching dog; in participant observation the question is decided, by and large, contextually (Fletcher, 1966).

When I returned from university to my new police posting my 'First' was, I suspect, bristling somewhat. The senior officers who welcomed me had rather different preoccupations. They did not seem to know much about where I had been during my absence from operational policing; neither did they know or think much about my subject. If I was glowing with academic pride, the senior officer of my new station was critical about the bristles I now sported. One greeted me with the words: 'The last thing I want is men with beards. I spend half my time telling men to get their hair cut'; and he continued, 'You will have no time for research. We have to get on with policing the ground and haven't time for experiments. What I want is people who can lead men.' I left my initial interviews with senior staff feeling intensely frustrated, hurt and not a little angry. Despite having read numerous articles on the methods of participant observation, not least on ways of gaining access to research, I found myself torn between opportunities for research and commitment to the police service, which had sponsored me at university. But such a beginning was parabolic; ethical decision-making about research is rarely a dispassionate, wholly objective enterprise.

It took me some time to perceive the pertinency of what the senior officers were telling me. When they said I should 'get into policing again' they were urging me to rediscover the 'common sense' of police work – the very theme of my research and of some current developments in the sociology of policing. The work of Cain (1973), Skolnick (1966) and Westley (1970), for example, indicates that the legal framework of policing shields a rather different practice; the lower ranks possess the organizational power to ensure that they retain a very considerable measure of discretion. I now found myself in a situation in which I could probe the occupational culture in a unique manner, adding to this body of knowledge.

After weighing all the options – requesting permission for research access from Headquarters and/or from my lower-ranked colleagues, resignation and so on – I decided to begin my field-work by adopting a covert strategy. From the available evidence this seemed the only realistic option; alternatives were either unrealistic or involved an element of the unethical, which would have rendered them only marginally more commendable than covert observation. Further, as a legally empowered police officer I was a member of a powerful institution of our society who would deal, though not exclusively, with the less powerful. The argument that all individuals have a right to privacy (that is to say, freedom from observation, investigation and subsequent publication based on the investigation) is strong but should be qualified when applied to the police. Research and my previous experience of police work demonstrated the power of the lower ranks, not least their resistance to external control of their work.

Any effective research strategy would have to pierce their protective shield if it was to be successful.

This problem is encountered during research of many organizations; however, the case for covert research is strengthened by the central and powerful situation of the police within our social structure. The police are said to be accountable to the rule of law, a constitutional constraint which restricts their right to privacy but which they can neutralize by maintaining a protective occupational culture. When such an institution is over-protective, its members restrict the right to privacy that they possess. It is important that they be researched.

It may be pointed out that this argument neglects the supervisory work of managerial officers. However, at Hilton this control is fairly minimal. It would have been highly restrictive simply to place one's data in the hands of senior officers, believing that they would or could straightforwardly alter the practices of policing by lower ranks (Chatterton, 1979; James, 1979; Mechanic, 1962). The covert researcher of the police has to be reminded that he is working within an extremely powerful organization which begs revelation of its public and private face by first-hand observation — risky as that observation might be. In part, therefore, my covert research is justified by my assessment of the power of the police within British society and the secretive character of the force. This does not mean that covert research into powerful groups is ethical while that into less powerful ones is not (Young, 1970); neither is it advocate a sensational type of sociology in which rigorous analysis of evidence gives way to moral crusading. Although I came to this uncomfortable conclusion when my research began ten or more years ago, I would still argue in similar terms, despite widespread changes in police policy.

Defining the limits of research

Having made the decision in principle to conduct covert research, I had to face its practical implications and responsibilities. This was none the easier for my being a police sergeant, holding all the legal powers of that office as well as being responsible for the supervision of a large number of officers who would be working according to their 'street-wise' rules. I was not a sociology lecturer masquerading as a schizophrenic, an alcoholic, a millenarian, a Pentecostalist or a factory worker; I was actually a police sergeant who had no idea when or if he would leave the field for other work (Festinger *et al.*, 1956; Homan, 1980; Loftland, 1961; Rosenhan, 1973; Roy, 1960).

Unlike experimental, questionnaire and other controlled methods, covert research is equivocal; those who are being researched control the situation as much as, if not more than, the researcher. When the subject of research is the police, whose job is highly unpredictable and varied (no less so when the researcher is a serving police officer), the definition of the limits of ethical tolerance is a significant matter. Codes of ethics like those adopted by the professional associations for social scientists deal with predictable and planned research, with conditions which are not present in fieldwork – indeed, their absence is the very reason why naturalistic methods are chosen (British Sociological Association, 1973).

During my first days of police duty I asked myself what I would do if, as happened in the case of another researcher of the police (Westley, 1970, p. viii), an officer hit a suspect in my presence or some other indiscretion took place. I was, I kept reminding myself, not simply a sociologist but a sergeant with supervisory responsibilities (Westley, 1970). Contemplating ethical problems which *might* arise hampered my capacity to document in detail. However, the police unknowingly provided me with a pilot study through which I was able to learn how to handle such issues – or so I thought – before being transferred to another station. My Chief Divisional Officer posted me to a small station where, with two other sergeants, I was responsible for about twelve constables. During my first week's duty I worked as station officer. I recorded the following incident:

> A man was arrested for driving whilst unfit through drink, and I dealt with the charge. He was exceedingly uncooperative, and I suspected that sooner or later he would be hit by a police officer; I took firm control of the situation. For a brief period the prisoner was alone with me, and he suddenly made a dash for the door, finding it incorrectly unlocked, and ran for the street. I shouted and gave chase, catching him and bringing him back to the charge room. As I returned him, other officers arrived.

The rules of the occupational culture direct that a loss of police control like this should be redressed by physical contact, but I did not offer that contact, and my colleagues saw that I did not. In this way I began to define the limits of their and my tolerance but recorded only the most cursory of field notes.

Three nights later I dealt with a man who had threatened his wife with a pistol. He pleaded his innocence, and a police officer kicked him on the backside, not with excessive force but just to remind him that his explanation was not acceptable. The incident was recorded, but I omitted from my notes the fact that the prisoner had been kicked; for good or ill, it was too sensitive an issue for me to accept. Similar situations arose, and I recorded in my diary:

> It is still a problem working with another police officer who has very different ideas about civil liberties − patrolling with Sergeant − , in this case. Every time we stopped someone I had to manage a situation in which the possibilities of corners being cut were real. This causes a strain for the sociological observer.

I was that impersonal observer; the realization that I was actually involved in grappling with such ethical issues was slow to dawn. But incidents like these were not the only experiences that informed my covert research. I also gained access to, and recorded, very private and − I do not use the word lightly − precious moments of people's lives. One day a mother called the police after the sudden death of her young baby. In her grief-stricken state she made some remarks about her marriage − I did not record them. I recall wrapping the baby in a blanket and holding it in my arms as two silent colleagues drove with us to the mortuary. The mortuary attendant took the child and, in a routine fashion, placed it in a refrigerator. One of my colleagues said that he felt like 'putting one on' the attendant for the way he treated the child. I later classified the conversations about the incident as jokes and stories; they proved to be the genesis of an idea about the use of humour in managing the personal stress of police work. I should also add that incidents like this reminded me of the demanding work required of the police, and of their humanity − I needed to be reminded of that.

The first couple of months of research were exceedingly

tough. Despite support from my academic supervisor, I could not make much sense of the data that I was collecting. I applied for an academic post which, thankfully, I did not get. The PCs had noticed that my ideas about policing were rather different from their own. (When tea mugs belonging to the shift were changed we were presented with colours to suit our personality: my mug was yellow. 'Why yellow?' I asked naively. 'Because you're scared.') Senior officers found me truculent, and my chief doubted my suitability for the police service. I later complained of his insensitivity to another senior officer, who responded: 'You might disagree with Mr – , but do you disagree with 99 per cent of the officers at the station?' He explained, 'There are two important things about police work. First, policemen must be willing to cut corners or else they would never get their job done. Secondly, it's because policemen have been happy to gild the lily that the law has been administered in this country.' He was right. On these points I did indeed disagree with him, and he knew it. A new officer soon came to command my division, and he transferred me from my station and pilot study in participant observation to a new subdivision and, unknowingly, to the beginnings of a substantive research project.

My new station was much larger, and I now worked with an inspector, three other sergeants and about twenty-five constables. From the outset it seemed to me important to tell my colleagues about my attitude to the use of force and to the manner in which evidence is gathered, suspects are handled in the station and so on. This was often done by engaging them in conversation about a particular issue or job in which they were involved. For example, one of my fellow sergeants was known to use 'unorthodox techniques' when questioning suspects. When we chatted about this issue he gave me a full description of what he was and was not willing to do, citing examples to illustrate each point. His explanations proved to be very useful because I was able to compare his accounts with his subsequent behaviour and that of others. Fortunately, he enjoyed discussing such issues and drew on my opinions about sociology; he became an important informant, who was always happy to provide details of the actions of particular officers and of particular incidents.

I had began to define my limits of tolerance; immediate colleagues did not exclude me from information about their actions and enabled me to remain on the fringes of incidents which I found questionable. It was noticeable that PCs who brought a 'dodgy job' into the charge room would, if they had a choice, ask a colleague to deal with it; sergeants also intervened indirectly – they almost protected me – if they thought that I might spoil or misunderstand a procedure they wished to control. Eliciting accounts of what was going on in these situations was never difficult. The senior officers now began to air rather different views about me, and I found that I had settled (if that was ever the case) into my police and research work as a covert participant observer.

Stress – the life blood of participant observation

William Whyte (1955, p. 317), in his account of research in 'Cornerville' writes: 'I also had to learn that the fieldworker cannot afford to think only of learning to live with others in the field. He has to continue living with himself.' Covert research and the ethical questions it raises create conditions of stress within which the sociologist has to live with himself. For example, tension resulted from working with officers who did not share my values and assumptions about policing. Such, it might be said, is the nature of a nasty world; but I had some direct responsibility for the manner in which these officers behaved. I occasionally retreated from conversations and incidents over which I had no control and which I found distasteful. At times I had to deal with an officer whose behaviour exceeded the bounds of what I considered reasonable conduct. These situations could easily get in the way of research and increased the pressure of my work.

Then the constant reflection involved in participant observation added to the pressure of working in a busy station. Gold (1958) and others who have written on participant observation encourage us to consider a continuum with overt and covert observation and participation at either end. This conceptualization is too straightforward. In my covert research a constant triadic dialogue took place between the balancing of personal ethical limits, the aims of research and my duty as a police officer. There were times when research suffered because I was engrossed in police work and times when police work took second place to the recording of detailed evidence. The resulting tension was demanding and wearing.

The risk of 'going native' was always present, and at the beginning of each tour of duty I reminded myself of my research and its themes. There were days when I was less attentive than usual; but when I became too involved in policing I was often pulled back by a particularly distasteful event. On one occasion, after hearing a conversation about race relations, I wrote in my diary:

> I reacted badly to the conversation yesterday and want nothing to do with such sentiments. I remember saying to myself, 'Underneath, these policemen are ruthless and racist'. I seem to have slipped into the mould easily during the last couple of weeks and wonder if I should have been so easy with my feelings. The balance of participant observation is one which can so easily be submerged and forgotten. Now it has been brought before me in glaring lights, and all the old issues of ethics – when to speak out, how involved one should get, whose perspective one takes on – loom large. (Simon Holdaway)

quote about part. ob.

Finally, as a covert researcher of the police I was documenting the work of people who regarded me as a colleague. The risk of being found out was always present and I had to be sensitive to any indication that others – sometimes friends – might know what I was doing. I kept shorthand notes on a scrap of paper in the back pocket of my trousers; if I had to leave the station or charge office to make notes, I listened for approaching footsteps. Certain incidents had made me sensitive to discovery:

ethics + morals difficult situation risk of being found out

> While at the station I telephoned my supervisor to arrange a tutorial. After returning to the communications room a constable said to me, 'Switch that tape recorder off, sarge.'
> I asked, 'What are you on about?'
> 'Oh nothing.'
> I do not know what was meant and never found out, but this remark caused me considerable anxiety.

When these considerations are added to the sheer physical effort of policing – shift work, overtime, discordant leave days – the stress of covert research cannot be avoided: it has to be managed to the advantage of the researcher. I used my situation

stress – police research

to heighten my consciousness of what was going on around me, not least when potentially stressful incidents were likely to happen. For example, I was able to make a particular study of police use of physical force, finding that I could tolerate its use more satisfactorily if I took detailed notes. This enabled me to check officers' attitudes against their actions, while clarifying the limits of my own tolerance.

Furthermore, as Bettelheim (1943) demonstrated in a situation that was far more extreme than my own, research can be a strategy for personal survival. I remained in the police for one year after my appointment as a lecturer at Sheffield University. Knowing that I would be leaving for a base from which I could publish and perhaps influence policy, research became more central to the task of making sense of my present and future positions.

Validity and reliability

If a research method is shot through with error, it is unsuitable for the documentation of any group. If the researcher is working alone, unable to hold research conferences with colleagues in the field, and is, so to speak, an apprentice, the problems of reliability and representativeness are considerable.

I worked on the basis of the straightforward premise that as much as possible should be observed and recorded, even the seemingly routine and insignificant. Further, data would be gathered on as many officers and in as many contexts as possible. Of course, published research helped to direct my attention to specific issues. Maureen Cain's (1973) work was very helpful to me at this point, as was the fact that I spent two years on field-work and did not have to complete a 'smash-and-grab' ethnography. Documenting over a considerable period of time enables the comparison of attitudes and actions in apparently unconnected but, in the light of subsequent analysis, interrelated events.

Rhetorical questions became very useful tools of analysis. If I was working on a particular theme, I would test my interest by questioning a number of officers:

One Sunday night I was patrolling with a colleague when a call to a fight came over the radio. The location of the call was too far away and the incident too trivial for a sergeant to attend, but we drove towards the scene at high speed. I asked my colleague: 'The only reason you drove like that was because you wanted to have a fast drive?'

He replied, 'Yes, well, it's a bit of fun, isn't it? It all makes a bit of excitement and gets rid of a headache.'

This reply offered some verification of a theme that I had been considering and was able to continue developing: similar means were used throughout the research.

Knowing what colleagues think of you is not always pleasant, yet the participant observer who elicits the views of those whom he is researching can use their opinions to discriminate between more and less reliable details of evidence. Academic supervisors required me to reflect on my data away from the bustle of the station, but, just as important, police colleagues tended to make their opinions known, usually by way of a joke:

In response to two exceedingly conscientious British Transport policemen, a colleague remarked, 'Right couple of lawyers we've got out there. They're trying to decide who cautioned him before he was arrested. Must have a sociology degree from Lancaster.'

On another occasion a constable said to me, as he left the canteen, 'I'm going to get a spade now, sarge.' He punched a fist in the palm of his hand.

These sorts of remark appeared to confirm my impression of other officers' attitudes and likely actions in situations that I witnessed and heard about.

Finally, although I have tried and found Schutz's (1962) member test of validity wanting, I have relied on police officers enrolled in extra-mural courses to comment on my work. To a lesser extent, I consider my own membership of the police relevant to the validity of research findings. One incident will illustrate this point. On one occasion, after chasing a number of suspects who had committed a burglary, I returned home to my wife (I had been off-duty, unloading shopping at the time the suspects appeared), raging about what I would do to them if they were caught. I was at that moment completely 'native', displaying all the attitudes of normal policemanship. In short, the experience of being a policeman is valuable in sustaining the empathy necessary to research founded on participant observation. *conclusion*

Into Civvie Street: analysis and publication

Leaving the police service proved to be a comparatively comfortable move, but it has left a nagging doubt in my mind: as I publish, I may hurt those who have unknowingly co-operated in my research. I agree with Roy Wallis (1977) that a sociologist owes this subjects 'an obligation not to cause them undeserved harm'. Guarding against 'undeserved harm' is very difficult; I circumvent the sanction of the Chief Officer when I publish and have already commented on why I do so. *guilt of part. ob.*

In this book all names and places have been changed in the cause of anonymity, and steps have been taken to ensure the security of the data. This measure is intended not to neutralize any officer's moral responsibility, including my own, but rather to enable me to take a broader view. Writing about the police, making my data available to pressure groups, giving evidence to official inquiries and other means of engaging in attempts to change police policy provide a continuing context for working through the moral issues posed by my research and my responsibility for its covert nature.

A risk of damage to the sociological community also has to be considered: it could be said that sociologists cannot be trusted. *quote* As yet I have not been subjected to such criticism from those who have commented on my work. Criticism may be forthcoming. I tend to the view that senior officers may permit research to refute my own findings and will therefore encourage further research work. (Any such studies would have to come to terms with the powerful masking of much police practice by lower ranks.)

Covert researchers therefore take risks when they publish their work: they risk the charges that they are simply engaging in a polemical exposé of an easily accessible 'whipping boy' and that their data are unreliable; they risk the possibility of action for attempting to convey the truth about a powerful institution in British society; they risk the consequences of a calculated deception of trust. I have attempted to argue that my research is based

risk of publication

looking back

on reasoned and acceptable ethical decisions. These decisions do not sanction research into any group of people. The question we should ask when deciding on any research strategy is this: 'If I were to place myself in the situation of those whom I wish to research, would I object to the covert method?' If we begin from this question and pit our evidence against it, preferably in debate with others concerned with the research, a good decision may well be made. In the end the individual researcher may have to make the decision to adopt a covert stance, accepting the risks that it involves. You will judge my work on the evidence presented to you and will come to your own conclusions about the methods used to collect it. For me there remains much truth in Whyte's remark that the sociologist has to live with his decisions.

important remark.

2

The Sociology of Police Work

As I recall the dilemmas encountered in covert research, I hear a voice coming from over my left shoulder, saying: 'You miss the point. Your research is directed towards the wrong issues. This apprehension you describe is not inevitable.' Together with other sociologists, Maureen Cain has hinted that the organizational level of analysis, like its academic survivals, is a matter of dealing with secondary issues – 'the icing sugar on the cake' (1979, p. 157). Priority, she continues, should be given to research dealing 'with fundamental issues, with the chemical processes which make the cake [of policing] possible at all' (ibid.). 'Police, then, must be defined in terms of their key practice. They are appointed with the task of maintaining the order which those who sustain them define as proper' (ibid., p. 158).

This argument is consistent with the attempt to develop a Marxist theory of deviance and social control, but, along with similar arguments, the desire for theoretical clarity surely throws us back upon the organizational studies that are criticized (Centre for Research on Criminal Justice, 1975; Hall *et al.*, 1978; Taylor, 1981; Taylor *et al.*, 1973, 1975). It is feasible to define police in terms of their 'key practice', but the notion of 'key practice' can be finally determined only by empirical description and analysis of the police at work, ideally by an ethnography.

Further, it may well be that what are called 'the chemical processes which make the cake [of policing] possible at all' are to be located outside the formal institution of the police. But if this is demonstrable, the relationship between the police and other institutions will ideally be assessed partly on the basis of evidence called from participant observation of the police at work.

Cain's reminder that, like all organizations, the police are situated in a social order within which power is unevenly distributed cannot be brushed aside. Neither can social theory be neglected. However, even if the type of research emphasis that Cain advocates is to be sustained, small-scale organizational studies remain a crucial and continuing source of our understanding of the police in Britain.

Another difficulty is that we have little more than a growing but still rudimentary knowledge of policing in Britain, and this is the case even if we accept the relevance of literature that is subsumed under the heading of 'Anglo-American policing'. Detailed analysis of some American studies which have formed the foundations of the sociology of the police in Britain reveal hitherto unrecognized ambiguity and insecurity. These studies direct us, once again, to the need for detailed ethnographies of the police at work as they patrol the streets and administer their array of legal and other resources in a multitude of complex situations. My apprehension about covert research may be justified.

American research

When American sociologists first asked the police that piercing research question, 'Hello, hello, what's going on here then?' they confirmed that in situations of clear illegality rank-and-file officers often choose to not enforce the law (Goldstein, 1960; La Favre, 1965; Packer, 1964). The reasons for these discretionary decisions, and the knowledge on which they were based, remained unknown. However, full law enforcement seems virtually impracticable. This early evidence of police behaviour has encouraged other sociologists to ask if deviations from legal directives (and, further, from internal policies) represent an adaptation of, and an accommodation with, conflicts arising from the organization of policing as much as, if not more than, blind indiscipline, conspiracy or whatever.

Two classic American studies, those by William Westley (1970) and Jerome Skolnick (1966), illustrate the effects of conflicts like these, emphasizing the important relationship between the police, the public policed and other organizations. Here the police organization is understood as an arena within which various definitions of 'proper police work' are moulded into a working model of policing. This working model is related more to the *perceived* demands from various sources made on lower ranks than to the *formal* demands of law or policy. The discretionary decisions discovered in the early research should be understood not as deviations from, but as examples of, normal policing. It would therefore be foolhardy to assume, even if the law were refined and clarified to ease the burden of enforcement, that the intentions of legislation or of any police instrument would be retained in the process of their translation from the written word to police action on the street.

Westley seeks to explain why the police of a small American town work in the aggressive fashion that he observed. This question directs him to two issues. The first is the patrolman's experience of meeting members of the public 'in their evil, their sorrow, and their degradation and defeat.... He sees this public as a threat. He seldom meets it at its best and it seldom welcomes him ... and for him they have no love' (1970, p. 49). The public is the policeman's enemy. Secondly, the police response to this hostility is aggression, considerable violence and a certain disregard for propriety, which feeds back into the existing frustrations and tensions of the public that is policed. So Westley's police are secretive and protective, placing the public at a distance. A sense of danger pervades their work, as does cynicism and aggression.

For Westley the police organization is directed not by legal and administrative rules to which police actions approximate but by a series of interpretations by lower ranks which vie with legalistic and other rules. The norms of policing – the occupational culture – are not derived from legal criteria of competence but fired and processed in the relationship between the police and the public.

Skolnick's *Justice Without Trial* acknowledges a debt to the ground prepared by Westley. Although he finds the locus of police conflict to be the tensions between the requirements of law and those of order, which are heightened by particular police policies, Skolnick retains the perception of danger and a hostile working environment so central to Westley's study. A 'working personality' is fostered as police work is informed by a sophisticated corpus of knowledge, attitudes and actions, which leads Skolnick to describe the policeman as 'craftsman rather than legal actor . . . skilled worker rather than . . . civil servant obliged to subscribe to the rule of law' (1966, p. 231). Elsewhere he suggests that patrolmen 'seem to be influenced more than anything else by overwhelming concern to show themselves as competent craftsmen' (ibid., p. 111). The basis of police craftsmanship is identified with the occupational culture.

The combined researches of Westley and Skolnick form much of the backbone of American research on the police. However, although they direct us to the importance of the occupational culture and the observation of police at work, their findings are ambiguous: the foundations that these scholars have laid may not be as secure as their disciples think. It seems that the police response which they document is a 'social construction' rather than a precise reflection of the situation facing officers (Berger and Luckman, 1967).

An ambiguity is apparent if we examine the evidence that Westley presents in the light of the assertion that hostility towards the police is most likely to be displayed by the Negro population. ('Negro' is the term used by Westley; in this book the term 'black' is used because it is part of the common verbal currency of Hilton's police.) There is certainly no evidence of blanket condemnation of the police by Negroes; the clearly documented reciprocal hostility expressed by the police can therefore hardly be justified. Of the small sample of thirty-five Negroes interviewed, nine thought the police were doing 'an excellent job', seven 'a fair job', eight thought them 'rude', seven considered them 'corrupt' and a further seven thought that the police were controlled by the local political machine. Four stated that Negro policemen have no authority (1970, p. 54).

Clearly Westley has divided some replies into more than one category, and it is therefore impossible to establish the internal consistency of each interview. Nevertheless, his interpretation of the replies seems over-stretched. In the light of the fact that the most significant numerical indicator of the Negroes' perception of the police suggests a largely favourable view, how can it be concluded that 'it is clear that among even the more prominent Negroes rough treatment at the hands of the police is not unusual and that in the Negro community no love is lost on the police force' (ibid.)? These data should be placed alongside the very strong evidence of 'anti-Negro' feeling among the large police sample interviewed, only 24 per cent of which expressed positive sentiments towards the Negro population.

Similar points could be made about all the groups that Westley questioned. We find on the one hand a very mixed set of public responses, which are indicative of a range of attitudes to the police, and on the other a framework of attitudes from a sample of policemen who (there can be little doubt) perceive the public as hostile. Westley's valuable research therefore begs the question of how the police construct a sense of hostility from the vast range of diverse experiences encountered during the course of their routine work.

A similar criticism can be made of Skolnick's work. He relies on Westley for much of his description of the 'working personality' but presents very little evidence that this is moulded in the course of routine police work. However, even if Skolnick's officers face a dangerous working environment, there is evidence to suggest that they find this situation a desirable and normal one. When asked which job they would most like to have in the police department, 50 per cent of the large sample named that of detective, 37 per cent cited patrol work, 8 and 4 per cent respectively named the juvenile and administrative sections (1966, p. 47). These preferences can be interpreted in terms of the diminishing levels of danger that they present to the personnel involved. Again, we come to the suggestion that this perceived danger is constructed and sustained by officers in the course of their routine work. The question of how such a perception of police work is constructed and sustained leads us back to the need for an ethnography of urban policing as it takes place on the streets.

British research

Although slight in quantity, research of the British police leads us to these same questions. Following Michael Banton's (1964) seminal work, Maureen Cain's (1973) doctoral research has provided a description of policing in an urban subdivision. She found that constables were oriented primarily to crime-fighting, a task which in fact formed a very minor part of their working day. The act of making an arrest for a criminal offence was, in their eyes, the central act of 'good policing' and the primary example of proper police work. However, because such arrests were infrequent occurrences, drunks tended to be arrested to foster the partial experience of 'authentic' policing. The primacy of arrest was related to the need for action which the constables expressed, and the chase, capture, fight and scuffle before an arrest were equally central to their definition of police work.

Times between bursts of action, defined by officers as boring times, led them to seek places where they could get a cup of tea, sleep, or chat with people in similar occupations or with colleagues. Because 'easing' was contrary to the internal disciplinary code of the force, the lower ranks were dependent upon each other for the retention of secrecy. Secrecy was necessary, therefore, to protect individual officers from the possibility of internal discipline and also to shield them from public accountability. The circumvention of formal rules was thought desirable, and the protective secrecy of the lower ranks sustained this view. In short, the work group provided the primary source of role definition.

Maureen Cain's description of the occupational culture provides an initial point of reference for my own research; much of what she identifies remains highly relevant to urban policing. My work extends her description into areas previously uncharted by research and takes into account the effects of two changes in the organization of policing: first, the 'unit beat' scheme of policing which was in use at Hilton and, secondly, the increasing emphasis on the police as members of a profession, evident among the senior ranks of Hilton's force. In the context of these changes I ask how such a particular view of policing is constructed and maintained by lower ranks.

This concern comes close to that of more recent work by Chatterton (1975a and b) and Manning (1977). Manning argues that the external appearance of what he calls 'Anglo-American policing' is rather different from the internal reality; this tension prompts him to organize his material on the police around the 'dramatic metaphor'. However, it is difficult to know how to read his book *Police Work: the Social Construction of Policing*. Is it a study in organization theory, a speculative work or a partial ethnography? The sheer ambition of his project leads to the tenuous linking of findings from many different research projects, as if they could all be easily related to illuminate his new understanding of policing. In fact, Manning's argument points to the *possibility* that much policing is symbolic rather than instrumental (if such a distinction is feasible anyway) and demands further study to document how, in contemporary policing, officers actually employ mechanisms of dramatic performance. The call for close observation of policing remains.

Once we steal a glimpse of a gap between the surface appearance of policing and a rather different underlying reality, successive layers of police folklore can be pared away. Studies of British and American policing have begun to do just this; however, the further question of how the gap between appearance and reality is sustained in the course of routine police work has not been answered.

We know that a concern with crime is a pervasive feature of the rank-and-file view. However, we also know that most police work is concerned with 'peacekeeping' and 'police social work' as much as, if not more than, it is concerned with crime (Morris and Heal, 1981, pp. 9–13). Similarly, lower ranks take the view that they are in the front line in the process of discovering and investigating crime – a view strongly challenged by many studies, which demonstrate that members of the public are crucial to every aspect of the detection of offenders (ibid., pp. 29–33). How, then, is this sense of the centrality of crime upheld in routine work? How is the view of the police as crime-fighters sustained? These questions incline us to the view that, in exploiting the contingencies of policing – a job in which end results are diffuse and imprecise and which necessitates discretion, low visibility and an ability to withhold information from senior ranks – the lower ranks construct, maintain and legitimize a definition of policing which seems to be at variance with the 'real' context of their work. So they unfetter themselves from legal and organizational constraints, and, as Peter Manning (1979) has put it, 'policing tends to be shaped by adaptations made by actors to structural patterns, to the reality they perceive, construct and maintain' (pp. 48–9).

This book is an ethnography of an urban police subdivision at work. It represents an attempt to map the police organization, laying bare the assumptions that officers make about their routine work (Schutz, 1970a and b, 1972, 1974). The description and analysis of the data (some repetition of which is unavoidable as themes are consolidated in later chapters) are ordered around what has been called the 'interpretive paradigm' (Wilson, 1971) and are influenced by David Silverman's (1970) argument that an organization should be conceptualized as an arena of action, 'a multitude of rationalities each of which generates the "in-order-to" motives of the participants and allows them to make their own sense of the actions and intentions of others' (p. 194). In constructing and sustaining (Berger and Luckman, 1966) their understanding and practice of policing, Hilton's officers retain the core of the occupational culture as a key resource for their work – which is our cue to go down to the station.

3

The Police Station

Walk through the front door of Hilton police station and you soon arrive at the station office counter. The station office itself is housed on the other side of this public counter; all the operational work of the subdivision is organized from here. Telephones ring, a teleprinter is typing and personal radios are being answered as you make your inquiry. Try to get beyond the counter and into the station itself – the charge room and cell area, for example – and you have a problem. The further you move from this small public area into the increasingly private world of the police station, the further you penetrate police-controlled space. The counter forms what Goffman (1969, pp. 32–40) has called a 'front', an area of space within which a particular public appearance is managed, shielding a backstage space where a rather different type of police work can be carried out. Hilton's officers routinely preserve the privacy of this backstage area to prevent their work from coming under public scrutiny (Holdaway, 1980).

A number of callers at Hilton can legitimately ask to pass beyond the counter into the private, police-controlled space; this sometimes causes problems. Some will want to advise or support a person held in custody; these visitors might be friends and relatives, solicitors or doctors (Zander, 1972). The consent of both the officer in charge of the case and the detainee is necessary before a move from public to private space can be made, a requirement that allows time for any necessary backstage preparations.

It is quite possible for an unintentional intrusion into private space to occur without the permission of an officer. A member of the public standing at the counter may overhear a private conversation between police officers in the station office, who may be discussing police matters. A management problem may arise if the stranger's presence is noticed.

Then there are those who are invited into police space by the police themselves; such people enter with some warning, and officers are able to anticipate the activity that they will find there. However, their early arrival can disturb or delay inappropriate policing. It is conceivable, for example, that a police surgeon called to examine a suspect will walk into the charge room just as some rather unorthodox techniques of questioning are about to begin.

Finally, moving away from visitors who may touch on the scrutiny and external accountability of the police to internal accountability to senior officers, it is possible for a senior officer to walk into a situation in which irregular behaviour is taking place. I am thinking here of the senior officer who has overall responsibility for the running of the station but whose direct intervention in its day-to-day work is fairly unusual. At Hilton, for example, he rarely if ever watches or supervises the questioning and charging of suspects. His intervention is generally concerned with the appearance of order and efficiency in the station itself, probably in the station office.

The station office

The station office is a very busy place; it is the operational core of the building and the subdivision. Books and papers are usually strewn over the station officer's desk, several telephones ring at once and his personal radio operates simultaneously. Add to this hubbub the work of the communications officer, numerous constables who want advice, a reference book or simply a chat during a break from patrolling, and the scene has the appearance of disorder rather than efficiency.

During periods when few demands are being made on the station officer – say, during the early-morning and other tea breaks – the station office becomes a gathering place for the whole relief. Officers sit on desks; cups are left in the office. Members of the public cannot see this informal scene because a screen of one-way glass faces them at the counter. The problem is that senior officers can visit the station office at any time.

In fact, their visits are rarely a surprise, and due warning is given to allow for the staging of an appropriate scene. The chief superintendent or superintendent always arrives between 8.30 and 9.00 each morning, and his first task is to check all entries in the books used by station officers during the previous twenty-four hours. Before his arrival the station office is tidied; cups and other evidence of tea-drinking are removed; and all staff are kept out of the office until he leaves. The temporary impression is one of tidy efficiency and managerial control as the station officer parrots, 'All correct, sir.' Yet the officer in charge of the station has risen through the ranks and knows that this is merely a performance staged for his benefit; he knows tea is prepared in the small writing-room adjacent to the office. (During an interview one young probationer constable called it the 'tea room'.)

Every weekend the whole of the division is supervised by one senior officer of at least chief inspector rank. He usually tours the division on Sunday morning, visiting every station to sign the books and perhaps to look at some other records of weekend work. Sunday morning is generally a time when PCs wash their private cars in the station yard; the station office is very untidy, the atmosphere very relaxed. Before the senior officer's arrival at Hilton a telephone call is generally received from his base station or from another station that knows of his impending visit. Hilton's station office is tidied; officers remove their cars from the yard; and the station sergeant ensures that they go out on patrol.

It is rare for a visit to be made during the late afternoon shift, but one Sunday a chief inspector from a neighbouring station walks into the station office without prior warning. The relief is drinking tea, and a television is on in an adjoining room. As soon as officers notice his arrival they begin to look busy: one picks up a piece of paper and walks through the office; another grabs a car log book and makes a hurried entry; a sergeant goes to work at his desk. Within seconds the office is cleared and becomes a 'front region'. The chief inspector says nothing.

Senior officers form part of the police team that stages this and other scenes of ordered supervision (Goffman, 1969, pp. 83–108; Manning, 1977, p. 28). They know that they can betray their subordinates but serve as both audience and actor during the contrived presentation of normality, masking the discrepancy between the activity in the front and the back regions. Of course, there are occasions when officers have to account for their presence in the station and times when the chief superintendent finds fault with the administration of the station office. Nevertheless, within the accepted framework of legitimate practice, senior officers expect a performance in the office and are tolerant if they realize that insufficient warning has been given to allow the officers to construct a tableau of operational efficiency. If mistakes are found during a set visiting time, failure to present the proper appearance of orderliness is grounds for criticism.

Team management is also required when members of the public at the station counter – the boundary between public and private space – are able to overhear conversations taking place in the body of the station office among officers discussing private aspects of their work. Two constables ask me and another sergeant about a case involving a girl who has bought a stolen car. They are arguing about their right to arrest her, and during the discussion a member of the public comes into the station and overhears what is being said. The constables do not realize that they are being indiscreet, and an inspector who notices the stranger intervenes.

A PC disagrees with the suggested arrest of the girl. 'No, you're on dodgy ground there.'
Colleague: 'We've had no more dodgy jobs than that in the last fortnight.
The inspector intervenes, 'Sh,' but the officers don't seem to understand him.
Sergeant: 'She's not a criminal. What do you want, just a red-ink stop, do you want to bring her in for that?'
'No, sarge, she's got a nicked car. She's got to be interviewed and brought in.'
The inspector intimates his unease: 'Ssh,' and the PCs leave the station.

In this situation the tentative character of police teamwork is highlighted, but notice how the highest-ranking officer invokes team discipline; he has to take ultimate responsibility for his colleagues. The man standing at the station counter probably does not understand the conversation taking place – he may not even be listening – but the mere presence of this stranger on the boundary between the public and private areas of Hilton police station threatens exposure of the views of lower ranks, which are seeping into an inappropriate public terrain.

The charge room and cell block

Suspects are brought into the secure and private space of the charge room after their arrest. They are searched, and all property is removed from them to the safe custody of the station officer. If they are to be charged with an offence, a brief procedure is followed, and they are either bailed or housed in one of the cells to await transport to the magistrates' court. The charge room is therefore a place where the police have considerable legal control over people – which is necessary and understandable. However, Hilton's officers assume more than legal control in this area of space. Once in their custody, a suspect is meant to comply with the directions that officers feel appropriate. They expect deference, quietness, compliance with searching, questioning, obedience in the charge room and composure (Chatterton, 1975b, p. 380). Their working assumption is that people who are brought to the station are 'prisoners' – that is their designation, not 'suspect', 'detainee' or 'person arrested'.

Secure from the presence of strangers, the charge room is a permanent 'home territory' (Lyman and Scott, 1967). Indeed, when policemen refer to Hilton they usually mean the charge room. To take someone 'down the nick' is to place them under police control; what happens next can vary, as a sergeant from another station once explained: 'As a general rule it has been my experience that in a police station a person gets as good as he gives. If he is co-operative, then the police are OK with him; if he is not co-operative, then he gets it.' For the lower ranks, the station *is* the charge room, a place where control can be maximized. Of course, there are limits to behaviour and rules of conduct to be observed, but essentially officers feel at home when they bring a 'prisoner' to Hilton; it is their place.

Contrary to regulations, if an arrest is made at a location just beyond Hilton's boundaries, the suspect may be returned to Hilton station. This boosts the station's arrest figures and maximizes the Hilton officers' control over the charging process. PCs know their own supervisory officers and the colleagues who might assist at some stage of the procedure; they feel more secure in this setting. Control is therefore focused on the charge room, for although police control may be tenuous on the streets, it is assured here. If their authority is resisted outside, the officers know that here they are relatively free to redress the balance, 'to give as good as they get', as the sergeant put it. Recalcitrant suspects are often told, 'You're in a police station now, you know.' Control in the charge room is the touchstone of a 'working police station'.

The charge room can also be a public place. If it is legal for Hilton's officers to take their suspects to the security of the charge room, it is also legal, given certain conditions, for the relatives and friends of these suspects to visit them. Many officers are suspicious of this type of intrusion. At a divisional instruction class the community liaison officer raises the issue of the staff of the local law centre seeking access to the charge room and cells. He explains to the sergeants in the class that if a person from the law centre asks to see someone who is detained, they should 'tell the prisoner that he has arrived and ask if the prisoner wants to see the person from the law centre'. He goes on; 'We have had cases where the solicitors are not wanted, so then you can tell them to leave, but you must ask the prisoner first.' Rather different attitudes are suggested by this record of a discussion:

PS 1: 'If the governors had backed us up against these people first of all and said no, we would have stopped all this business.'

PS 2: 'I think the best way to deal with this is to say that the prisoner doesn't want to see the solicitor.'

Chief inspector: 'Yes, but you must ask the prisoner first.'

PS 2: 'Yes, that is what I mean: "The prisoner doesn't want to see you." '

Others were less severe. One said: 'I have had these people come in and have found that the best way to take the wind out of their sails is to say, "Yes, sir, if you would just take a seat, I will tell the person that you are here." They don't know what is going on.'

During a night duty a youth is arrested for the possession of what are suspected to be illegal drugs. He telephones a legal

representative and asks for help at the station. I tell my assistant
station officer this, and he suggests that the solicitor 'doesn't get
past the front counter'. The inspector, who is listening, says:
'What's wrong with him, then? Got weird ideas, hasn't he?',
suggesting that he and other officers are quite willing to permit
solicitors and other persons to enter the charge room. However,
another incident in which this inspector is involved indicates
that although he is willing to allow solicitors into the charge
room, precautions to stage-manage the setting properly may have
to be taken before access is granted.

> A PC is about to arrest a juvenile who has come to the
> station with his father and a solicitor from the law centre.
> They are sitting in the foyer, out of hearing of the con-
> versation taking place between the inspector and the PC in
> the station office.
>   Inspector: 'Caution him. Tell him what you know and
> tell him you're arresting him and caution him again. Do it
> all properly, just do it all properly.' He then glances towards
> the people in the foyer and the boy is arrested.
>   As the parties move to the charge room, I hear the solicitor
> say to the youth, 'All right, don't answer any questions from
> now on, okay.' He also recognizes the different spatial
> settings within which the police work.

The presence of the solicitor ensures that the correct arrest and
charging procedure is followed, and the inspector takes care to
maintain a common police front of legality.

In fact, solicitors rarely arrive at the station soon after an arrest
is made, and the delay allows adequate time for preparation
should anything be awry. The police surgeon presents rather
more of a problem here because although he is always called to
examine a suspect who seems ill or is injured, the timing of his
arrival is more uncertain. The doctors who come to Hilton
regularly are not strangers, and officers know that they are
sympathetic to their work. Nevertheless, they are not directly
employed by the police and can cause considerable trouble if
they come upon a situation of near-illegality or question how or
when a suspect has sustained injury. It is therefore sometimes
necessary to prepare a setting before the doctor arrives.

Suspects with blood on their faces are asked to wash very soon after they arrive at Hilton – this makes their injury look less spectacular from the outset. A check may sometimes be made on a suspect who alleges assault during arrest. When a black youth is arrested a scuffle takes place, but it seems that very little force is used by the police. The youth's mother and sister come to the station and allege that he has been beaten up; they want a doctor to examine him. They are allowed to see the youth, and although he has no apparent injuries, his sister says:

'Look at the bruises and cuts on him. Look at them. Tell him you've been beaten up. Come on, don't be frightened. Tell him you've been beaten up. Who hit you? which one was it?' Shouting follows, and a fellow sergeant says he will get a doctor.

It is obvious that there is no injury to the boy, but despite this my colleague turns to the PC who made the arrest and asks, 'I'm going to get a doctor to examine him just to make sure nothing goes wrong at court. We won't find anything, will we?'

PC: 'No, I only struggled with him in the street, trying to arrest him.'

The check is made in case any unseen injury has been caused, and some management of the situation is required before the doctor's arrival.

Officers dealing with a suspect in the charge room sometimes find that a doctor who has been allowed past the station counter interrupts their inquiry. After a vicious fight, during which a suspect has been hit across the head with a truncheon, the suspect is told to wash the blood from his face and to answer questions. Two CID officers who are handling the case come into the charge room, and one of them begins to ask questions. At this moment the divisional surgeon walks into the room. A comment is made later: 'What a bastard that the doctor had to walk in at that time!' The implication is that his presence in the private space of the charge room inhibited aggressive questioning.

On another occasion a doctor walked in on a similar scene.
Officer: 'If Dr – hadn't come in just then, he would have got it.'
'Was he [the suspect] taking the piss?'

'No, not really. He was just awkward. He was all right when he first came in, but when he had the blood sample taken he got really difficult and awkward. He had another go just as he was leaving the station.'

'Yes, he knew he couldn't get hit when the doctor was there, and it was the same just then. He knew he could get to the door and get out quick.'

Although they are frequent visitors, doctors can present a threat to the privacy of the charge room. More trust is extended to the doctor than to the solicitor because the solicitor has a closer link with police accountability to the courts; nevertheless, the presence of doctors and solicitors in the charge room requires officers at Hilton to try to create and sustain an appearance of legitimacy for their work.

There are two further groups of people with access to the charge room – suspects and supervisory officers – whose status shields them from knowledge of police action which might border on illegality. Once in the charge room, a suspected person is normally taken to a supervisory officer, who hears the evidence of circumstances surrounding the arrest. This procedure should be, and usually is, an open one, enabling the suspect to answer any relevant questions or to comment on the evidence presented. However, changes are made if an arresting officer thinks he has a 'dodgy one'. A 'dodgy' job is a case in which the circumstantial evidence is slight or the arrest has been provoked by the behaviour of the suspect during initial investigations rather than by evidence of some other substantive offence. When a PC brings in a 'dodgy' job the open procedure can change to one of closed awareness (Glaser and Strauss, 1967) through the creation of private space within the charge room. The arresting officer speaks to the supervising sergeant as he walks into the station office and stands close to him, with his back turned to the suspect. Alternatively, he waits until the sergeant moves to stand behind the charge-room desk, leans over the desk to create greater privacy and then indicates that he wants to move from the charge room to some other place. This move helps to promote uncertainty in the suspect as well as a sense of police privacy and secrecy.

After arresting a number of juveniles for creating a disturbance in the street, the principal arresting officer begins to outline his rather tenuous evidence to the inspector supervising the charge. He suggests, 'Shall we go out of here?' and the discussion moves to the station office. Privacy and protection are ensured by this move into a new area. Some supervisory officers allow the whole charge room to be 'free space', remaining in some other part of the station until they think any possible illegality has ceased, as this incident illustrates:

> A station officer knew that a person who had assaulted two officers and had been involved in a vicious fight with the police was about to arrive at the station. I asked the telephonist who was on duty at the time if she knew how the station officer dealt with this situation. 'Well, he was playing cards, and when all the commotion was going on in the charge room he just continued playing cards and said, "We'll wait until it's all quietened down," and then he went down there and dealt with it.'

His deliberate non-intervention ensures the privacy of the officers in the charge room and avoids compromising the sergeant.

If unorthodox techniques of questioning are to be used, two areas are considered suitable. One is private space created within the charge room:

> Five youths have been arrested. They are brought to the station for questioning and charging. It is not possible to split them up by putting them into separate cells or detention rooms, so the arresting officers create privacy within the charge room. [A short corridor leads from the door of the station yard to the body of the charge room. If prisoners are sitting on the bench in the charge room, they cannot see along this corridor.] While the boys are being questioned I walk into the charge room and notice that those seated on the bench look very frightened, far more frightened than when they first came into the station. As I move further into the charge room and am able to see along the corridor, I notice that one of the arresting officers is standing their with one of the suspects. I ask,
> 'What are you doing?'
> 'Well, he's just answering a few questions for me, sarge.'
> My intervention has stopped what I later learn to be unorthodox questioning of the youths.

A more usual ploy is to take the suspect from the charge room to the cells or detention room, away from other prisoners who might be in the charge room. The station officer often initiates this move, especially when a number of persons are arrested for the same offence. It makes the investigation more manageable but, more important, the use of isolated space increases the power of the police, reinforces the captive status of the suspect and is in itself a strategy of control.

Isolation is also used to increase the likelihood of confession. As he locks a suspected illegal immigrant in a detention room an officer explains, 'She's a liar and I want the truth to sink in a bit.' Even well known 'professional criminals' from Hilton are placed in isolation for the same reason.

> Such a suspect asked a constable, 'What's all this about?'
> Officer: 'I don't know. He [the officer in charge of the case] will be down to tell you in a minute. I don't know what it's about, mate. All right, just sit there for a moment.'
> The suspect was put in a cell. The arresting officer then telephoned his headquarters office to establish the evidence required to permit the suspect's continued detention. There seemed to be little, and it was suggested that he be taken to another station for questioning.
> 'Oh well, that's all we've got, is it? Well, I think we will just take him to Greenway and let him shit himself on the way over there.'

A threat of isolation is sometimes sufficient. An officer took a juvenile to the door of a cell passage and explained:

> 'That's where we put naughty boys like you [indicating the detention rooms]. But we put men, naughty men, over there, in those cells there. Do you want to go in one of those cells?'

He then took the boy to the door of a cell, returned to the charge room and a confession was soon obtained. Isolation is also made if submission to police authority is not forthcoming.

> Some juveniles were arrested for causing a disturbance in the street; a sergeant dealt with them after arrival at the station. One, a tall youth who was later found to have

nothing to do with the incident, appeared complacent. The sergeant told him, 'No, you don't sit down in here [the charge room], and you had better wipe that smile off your face or I'll do it for you. Come on, we had better deal with you in here.' He took the youth to a detention room.

Once in a detention room or cell, privacy is afforded the officers doing the questioning. The cells and detention rooms are known to be 'free territories':

'– [a CID officer] thumps them, but that's about all.'
'It always used to be that if you sent for the CID, the prisoner would get thumped around the cell, but it's not like that now.'

This reference to the spatial siting of violence is pertinent. Indeed, during her research Maureen Cain (1973, pp. 161–3) found a supervisory officer absenting himself from similar places where force could be used. She quotes him:

But then, from the charge room to the cells he [the arresting officer] had a chance to get his own back [on the suspect] and I don't blame him . . . I'd do the same. These people have got to be taught, you see.

The question of what actually happens in the cells is not the first concern here. The point is that cells and detention rooms are known as places where officers can free themselves from legal and formal organizational rules. The use of techniques which border on, and sometimes cross, lines of illegality leads to supervisory officers' knowledge of what is taking place in private space although they are not actually present. Any account of action within this space is a matter for as few officers as possible; error and contradiction are thus avoided, and the front of legality and managerial control is maintained.

Standing at the centre of the subdivision, Hilton police station provides a secure base from which officers go out to patrol. 'The nick' is secure in a number of different senses: it is necessarily secure to enable the safe custody of suspects; it is secure from public scrutiny of police work, not least within the charge room and cell areas; it is a safe haven in which officers can adapt law and policy to their own purposes. The further we move from the public space of the station counter into the increasingly private space of the station itself, the more dominant the values and practices of the lower ranks – the occupational culture.

Anyone unfamiliar with urban policing will be unable to find his way around the station with the ease of the constable and other ranks who work there. The routines that we have examined are directly related to police work as it unfolds in practice rather than as it is written into the law and formal police policy. For example, the boundaries between public and private space at the station office counter are patrolled because the teamwork and secrecy of the rank-and-file view has to be assured; the ways in which private space is carved out of the charge room permits the necessary protection required for the questioning of suspects in the manner that lower ranks think fit.

At one level, then, this description of the use and meaning of space within Hilton police station maps out how the members of an occupation construct their very specific world and protect it from outsiders. More than this, though, the documentation hints at many themes which will be laid bare in successive chapters of this book. Police work within the relative privacy and safety of the station is one aspect of a perspective and practice which is less securely worked out in the policing of Hilton's population. To understand this rank-and-file perspective more clearly it is necessary to begin to unravel both the central and the peripheral objectives of police work.

4

The 'Ground'

The area policed from Hilton station, the 'ground' as they call it, belongs to the police. They possess it; it is their territory and members of the force from adjoining stations have no right of entry into or patrol of the ground save by invitation, with the implied co-operation of Hilton officers or in pursuit of a suspect. During a tour of night duty a Bluecoat PC (Bluecoat is a sectional station attached to Hilton subdivision) is seen 'poaching' on Hilton section. A Hilton officer broadcasts a warning over the personal radio system, allowing all his colleagues to hear: 'Get off our ground. What are you doing on our ground?' The poacher replies, 'If you had enough policemen to police it, I would.'

Similarly, it is assumed that people working in allied organizations – social workers, fire brigade personnel, local authority officials – have no prior right of control over, or powers of intervention in, Hilton's territory without first acknowledging the primacy of police control. Of course, this notion of control is continually denied by all manner of disputes, disturbances and crimes and by the continuing work of these other organizations that deal with matters closely associated with police work; it is seemingly an impossible concept to uphold, contradicted by all external criteria of validation. Nevertheless, this view of Hilton as 'police-controlled territory' forms one central organizing principle of a mental map which officers use to order their work in the subdivision, a map that functions in a number of ways (Ball, 1973).

Ardrey (1966) has pointed out that territorial control is related to identity. The diffused and sometimes conflicting elements of the police role are rationalized as a coherent identity within this defined territorial area of the ground. Closely related to territory and identity is the relationship between territory and task. Claim to a territorial imperative imposes a unity on the myriad tasks which constitute police work. Hilton's police render their work identifiable, referable, traditional, routine and of importance to self. Finally, control of territory helps officers to make some sense of the negation of their supposed control. With the police map in mind, violation of control (natural and inevitable as that might be) may be understood as a challenge to the police and their symbolic status as guardians of the state. On the one hand, a rationale is created for policies which use the imagery of confrontation and, at times, virtual war against crime (Bittner, 1970); on the other hand, a world requiring vigilant control is a world which sustains the rank-and-file rhapsody of crime fighting, search, chase and capture, of action and hedonism.

The sense of Hilton as police-controlled territory is therefore crucial and closely related to another central notion, which is that of Hilton as poised continually on the brink of chaos. Unlike the American studies, which stress a pervasive sense of territorial danger (Rubinstein, 1973; Westley, 1970), Hilton's police perceive space, place and the local population as part of a world potentially erupting into disorder. No sense of conspiracy lies behind this view; Hilton simply remains on the brink of inevitable chaos, and the police save it from sliding over the edge.

While patrolling with an inspector, I pass a group of people who are standing on the pavement. The inspector comments, 'You can't rely on people behaving themselves nowadays. You know, any small thing triggers them off. It's really frightening.' Constables perceive the world in a similar way. On one occasion, during a conversation between two constables and myself, a more senior PC joined us from his car patrol:

'Yes, it's like a grave out there. (Pause) It's odd, this place is. You can go weeks really quiet, nothing happening at all, then all of a sudden, whoosh, it all happens, all hell let loose.'

The conversation shifted to a story about a prisoner being hit while he was being held in the police station for questioning. I asked a rhetorical question: 'I don't agree with all that [using physical force during questioning]. When policemen start taking the law into their hands, isn't there a great danger of law and order breaking down?'

The Constable replied, 'Well, it has broken down, hasn't it?'

He gained support and verification from a colleague: 'Yeah, it's broken down. It's absolute chaos out there.'

As far as the officers are concerned, these two apparently contradictory views – Hilton is 'really quiet' and 'It's absolute chaos out there' – are consistent. The inspector's remark, 'You can't rely on people behaving themselves nowadays', when commenting on a mundane scene, portrays the same perspective. Their implication is that if Hilton is on the brink of chaos, then its officers have a licence to intervene, using the range of remedies available, including their own strategies to prevent a slide into total disorder. Thus the uncertain, diffuse and conflicting nature of police work is rationalized.

It should be stressed again that this is not a conspiratorial view; rather, chaos is associated with a characteristic naivety among the population. Describing a constable who is thought to be poor at his work, a sergeant remarks, 'Well, he's just like a member of the public really, isn't he? He just doesn't think before he does anything. He's got no ability to weigh anything up at all. He's just like a member of the public.' Chaos and naivety go hand in hand; the police rationalize disorder into control, chaos into order.

These fundamental views form the basis of what Schutz (1974) has called the 'life-world' of the police. They sustain all other occupational values and beliefs, remaining when more peripheral ideas have been stripped away; they cannot be negated, since they form central axes of the police view of their role and the world in which it is played out.

Places to which particular significance is attached stand out as contours against this foundational background of control and chaos (Rock, 1974). Although officers do not demonstrate highly detailed knowledge of their territory, like that documented by Bittner (1967), they do acquire basic information about space and place which makes their work more manageable. Some status is attached to knowing one's way around the ground; knowing a location means being able to get to the action and excitement quickly. However, in the light of the primary realities of control and chaos, these other contours of spatial perception assume a more contextual form. Particular places – buildings and groups of buildings, small areas – stand out as relevant to the contingencies of policing as lower ranks understand them.

Sites of danger

Any place or area within Hilton subdivision can become a site of danger. During a period of IRA bombings of British targets the whole of the subdivision was pervaded by a sense of danger. But apart from such extreme situations, danger is not constant throughout the ground.

As far as Hilton's officers are concerned, just one place is constantly dangerous, demanding vigilance from the officers who visit it. This is a hostel for homeless black youths, many of whom have been convicted for criminal offences. It is noticeable that even visits to the hostel on trivial matters seem to threaten danger. Before a night-duty parade a PC is asked to inquire about a missing girl who is often there. Despite the very routine nature of the call, he asks for support from a car crew. On another occasion a constable requests assistance with a routine inquiry: 'I've got an inquiry at the hostel, sarge. All right if I take some-body with me? It's not that I'm a coward, but. . . .' Similarly, when a young black couple is seen arguing near the house, the car crew in the vicinity thinks that it might have to enter the building. A request goes out over the personal radio: 'There is nothing urgent, but we're probably going to have to go into the hostel and may need some assistance.' The hostel is regarded as a site of constant danger; this characterization arises from the primary realities of control and chaos.

Sites of trouble

'Trouble' has an internal and external dimension for the police (Chatterton, 1975b). External trouble means public opposition and the need for an account of police action, which is not welcomed. This notion of trouble is more relevant to Hilton's senior officers than to lower ranks.

The local law centre is a site of external trouble and an immediate point of reference for the officer in charge of my station. When welcoming me before my first tour of duty he stressed the opposition to police which the centre represents and assessed the credibility of a local black youth leader thus: 'He's not anti-police because he walked out of a couple of meetings which have recently been held by the law centre.' Of course, the law centre is typified as 'trouble' because its staff of legal assistants and solicitors have frequent contact with people who want to complain about police action. They know how to make complaints against the police and threaten to fracture the protective secrecy of the work group by asking to visit clients in cells or in the charge-room area of the station soon after arrests are made.

Another place of trouble for the chief superintendent is the local stadium of a First Division football team. As he sees it, his reputation is at stake if disorder occurs during a match and officers act inappropriately in front of television cameras and thousands of spectators. During my first day of duty at the station a colleague explains, 'After you have been here for a bit, sarge, you will find out that everything revolves around [the football ground]. . . . If you make mistakes down here, you might as well leave the subdivision or resign.'

At times quite stringent precautions are taken to identify and define an area of trouble because it has given rise to a complaint against the police. A woman who lives in a flat alleges she has had sex with a number of officers stationed at Hilton. The superintendent leaves a notebook for the station officer in which he is to report any telephone conversation he has with her; the same is done for the telephonist. Warnings are placed in the supervisory officers' 'informations' pointing out that trouble could arise if the woman telephones the station and an officer goes to the flat on his own. As soon as the allegations are withdrawn no further official attention is paid to the flat, and it no longer signifies 'trouble'.

In these cases there is the possibility that people will make trouble for the police by complaining about their actions, by drawing public attention to a disorderly situation, possibly by bringing the police into disrepute. The relevant spaces within which this potential for trouble is sited are clearly contoured against the foundations of control and chaos.

Although lower ranks dislike having complaints made against them and know that the law centre is a place from which complaints and critical comments come, they do not regard it with the same caution as do senior officers. Constables have rather different ideas about 'trouble'. To them 'trouble' means a short skirmish, a scuffle with drunks, an argument which borders on physical contact between police and public. There are places in the subdivision – public houses, for example – which are frequently the sites of trouble or disturbances, as they are officially called. This type of trouble can be fairly attractive. A PC broadcasts over the radio:

> 'It looks like there's going to be trouble at the Castle. Could a couple of units get along there? There's nothing happening at the moment but there might be trouble in a bit of time.'
> Personnel who have been to the scene return to Hilton after a short period and inform other PCs, 'You didn't miss much at the Castle. It was all over by the time we got there.'

The point is that 'trouble' like this offers lower-ranking officers an opportunity to enjoy a scuffle, to arbitrate authoritatively and perhaps to make an arrest for a minor offence. The occupational values of action and hedonism are woven tightly into the designation of spaces and places as troublesome.

Although external trouble can be fun, it can also rebound on lower ranks and become internal. Officers are often called to the local hospital casualty unit to deal with drunks, settle disputes and report accidents; the staff welcome them to do this. However, if the relationship between the police and hospital personnel is soured, the external trouble of action can lead to internal trouble associated with the accountability of the force.

After dealing with a number of people who have been taken to the casualty unit for treatment of injuries that may have been inflicted while they were held in custody, the hospital staff seem to discourage the police from entering the unit. A constable says that a doctor has asked, 'Is this another person who has been beaten up at Hilton police station?'

> On another occasion a person who has been struck on the head with a truncheon is admitted to hospital from police custody. He is under the usual police guard and during one tour of his 'guard duty' the officer telephones the station to say that some people are wanting to visit the injured man.

They seem highly excited and likely to cause a disturbance. Having dealt with the situation, the officer returns to Hilton and explains, 'The hospital are very "anti" at the moment with this bloke being beaten up. They won't co-operate at all because they don't like what's happened to him. He's only got a few bruises on the top of his head.'

The difficulty here is that the usually benign designation of the hospital – to be elaborated later – is changed to 'trouble'. Police action is now being constrained, viewed with suspicion, and the common sense of the occupational culture is open to possible scrutiny. Both the internal and external meanings of the term 'trouble' threaten the occupational culture: first, there is the risk that informal police practices will become visible; secondly, the interdependency of the work group may become strained.

Sites of work

A new sergeant has been posted to Hilton. We pass one of the hospitals as I drive him around the ground on his first day of duty. He asks me, 'Do we take the casualty?' I answer, 'Yes.' He says, 'Oh, that's work then.' Later that morning another sergeant describes the area to him. In the course of his description he refers to the two hospitals, 'which cause a lot of aggravation'.

Why do sergeants designate hospitals 'work' and 'aggravation'? As we have seen, hospital casualty units involve the police in the reporting of accidents, sudden deaths and a host of other incidents. The citing of hospitals as places of work is connected with the writing of reports on these incidents, work that is regarded as trivial and, as far as the constables are concerned, to be avoided. The sergeants are faced with the problem of persuading their officers to report incidents properly and, not least, to cover any possible criticism of their actions.

Constables may accept work at the hospital in order to enjoy the comforts of a warm place during a chilly night duty, but then they employ a tactic to avoid the work required of them – they tell the station officer that there is 'no cause for police action'. Alternatively, when the services of the hospital are not required by someone with suspected injuries, the constable's arrival at casualty can be delayed until the aggrieved party has left. However, hospitals outline a further contour, mapping out particular spaces in the subdivision.

'Mump holes'

In her research into urban policing Maureen Cain (1973, p. 37) describes places within the inner city where patrolling officers rest from, and relieve the tedium of, beat work. They drink tea or chat with the staff of cafés, pubs and other organizations. As Hilton is policed by car patrols, 'mump holes' (places where rest and refreshment can be obtained) seem to be unnecessary. In part, this is because the many patrol vehicles are warm and dry; constables frequently take a lift to break the monotony of their foot patrols, minimizing the need for extra resting places. A sergeant compares his experience of being a constable before car patrols were introduced. After he had 'tipped them out of the nick at 6.30 a.m.', as he puts it, 'when I was at Queen's Square and it was early turn, we had a full breakfast and a couple of cups before eight, and it was then time for tea at the nick. Our blokes don't even know where to go; Tom might, but he's the only one.' Some of the older PCs certainly have their 'mump holes', and it is common knowledge that the hospitals, some pubs and certain organizations offer a cuppa and rest. Yet all of these places implicitly require a reciprocal exchange: nurses, caretakers, publicans and shopkeepers occasionally require prompt assistance with disorderly customers or patients. Further, some shops, usually take-aways, are known to be 'GTP' (good to police). Again, this relationship is not without implicit reciprocal obligations.

Sites of interest

Before each shift leaves the station for patrol the constables attend a parade, which at Hilton means congregating at one end of a locker room. During the parade the duty sergeant reads items from the parade book. Most entries concern premises left insecure at night, the addresses of people away for long periods of time, leaving their houses unoccupied, and infomation from officers providing details of activity that might be suspicious.

A bulletin of crime information is published every week, which also contains information about addresses of local criminals, areas where crime is being committed and so on. To the enthusiastic officer the bulletin and parade book could provide a great deal of detailed information for use in his daily work. However, it is noticeable that very few constables record any of the information given on parade or study the information bulletin. Duty sergeants taking parade sometimes remind constables of the value of actually recording some of it! Nevertheless, knowledge of places where crime might occur and other similar information which they have is considered personal and private. Details of sites of interest tend to be recorded in case something goes wrong and it appears that officers have done nothing. 'Trouble', we know, means 'covering your ass'.

Home territories

'Home territories' have been described by Lyman and Scott (1967) as 'places where regular participants have a relative freedom of behaviour and a sense of intimacy and control over the area' (p. 270). At Hilton sergeants and constables create home territories out of available space to secure the freedom and privacy that they believe are necessary for effective police work.

If it is not possible to get a suspect to a police station and privacy is required, officers with adequate occupational knowledge may carve out an area of private space for their work. An incident which involved a colleague and me illustrates the point:

> We stopped two males suspected of theft. As they walked along the pavement we noticed that one of them was carrying a radio. Initial questioning of the two proved unsuccessful, and they were brought in together by the police car. One of the suspects, a youth, began to cry, and my colleague said to him, 'Look, sonny, you can stop turning those tears on because you are lying. As soon as I get you in the back of that car you are mine, and I'll find out where that radio came from.'

Privacy and secrecy are assured in the police car, where a home territory can be created, if only for a brief period of time. On another occasion I was patrolling in a vehicle driven by the same colleague.

> We came across two PCs who had just arrested a black youth for possession of an offensive weapon and a minor assault on police. The youth was quiet after arrest and was placed in the back of the PCs patrol car for transport to the station. My colleague drove to the station at speed, explaining in a rather dramatic fashion, 'We'd better get down to the station quick so they don't beat him to death.'

I recorded a third incident:

> A PC was relating an account of an incident during which a suspect had to be questioned. 'Yes, that PC from – Division said, "I better have a word with that bloke," and we put him in the back of the car. The WPC who was sitting in the front said, "Well, I think I had better go now." '

Similarly, on another occasion, after the arrest of a youth who had assaulted a colleague, an officer recalled:

> I put – [a WPC] in our Panda; she was saying, 'Don't hit him', to – and – [names of officers]. We said, "Get in there and keep quiet." He was put in another car and her colleagues 'continued'.

Cars are home territories in two senses. First, they offer secrecy and security from the public. Secondly, they are secure from the gaze and control of supervisory officers. A sergeant from another station situated at a considerable distance from Hilton makes this second point clearly. I asked him what he did about PCs who used physical force on prisoners. He replied: 'Well, we don't have any of that in our station at all. I've told them that I won't have it. I'm not worried about what happens on the way to the station, but once we're in the station, that's it, nothing happens.'

These safe spatial areas are not part of the natural or built environment but aspects of the structured spaces recognized by officers at Hilton. The creation of these home territories can be related to the use of techniques of questioning and persuasion

which extend the legal boundaries of action permitted to the
police. Like sites of trouble, danger and work, home territories
require officers to have a very specific and precise knowledge of
the occupational culture, most certainly more specific than their
knowledge of the primary reality of policing. Knowledge of how
to create a home territory and the limits of acceptable action
within this space is therefore the result of a considerable period
of learning within the occupation. Once the knowledge has been
acquired, the occupants of a home territory are freed from some
of the possible restrictions that might be placed on their actions.

Body territory

A final definition of space that I want to consider is that associated with the body – the area immediately surrounding it, as
well as clothing and associated accoutrements (Goffman, 1972,
pp. 51–87; Sommer, 1959, 1966). To the police officer body
territory is virtually sacred; the sacred is not to be profaned. The
sanctity of uniform and body territory is associated with both the
personal safety of the individual as well as the stability of the
political state, symbolized by the office of constable.
     Again, this is an area to be distinguished from the built envi-
ronment, but it is one of the utmost relevance to policemen, who
regard the violation of body territory as tantamount to in-
surgency. The pervasive, primary meanings of chaos and control
become immediate and critical when violation endangers the
physical and symbolic space of, and around, the physical self.
While I was at training school a sergeant on a course with me
commented, 'If anyone touches a policeman he deserves to be
hung.' At Hilton the assumption is made that if an officer is
assaulted, physical force will be returned, even if that force is a
token to reinstate the sanctity of the symbolic self. A suspect had
become violent in the charge room of the station and had assaulted a constable by throwing a chair at him.

> I asked the officer who had been on duty as station officer at
> the time of the incident, 'What state was the prisoner in?'
>   Sergeant: 'Not bad, really. There was a token, but he
> wasn't really beaten up, not by any means.'

A symbolic token can amount to the use of considerable force against an offender. However, the central point is that if body territory is violated, the violation is redressed by police use of force.

Because a policeman's body is infused with symbolism, its potency as a vehicle of meaning can extend beyond his skin and clothing to the equipment associated with policing – the truncheon and police car, for example. By using these objects, an officer can transform the space surrounding him into an area directly under his control. The driver of a police car can cruise past a group of people standing on the pavement and stare at them fixedly, intending to extend control from his body and vehicle into the relevant space. Some officers leave their truncheons on the dashboards of their parked and unattended patrol cars; this ploy is particularly noticeable among uniform officers working temporarily in plain clothes. Others leave police caps or helmets on the back seats or parcel shelves of their own cars. First, this may indicate that they expect favourable discretionary treatment if stopped after committing a traffic offence. Secondly, such use of uniform and other instruments indicates that the space surrounding the object is under police control. It is almost as if the police officer who owns the items was present and controlling the space. This understanding of body territory, associated with a more broadly accepted notion of proximity and touch within Western society, enhances the police sense of identity and power.

Throughout this description and analysis of space a close relationship has been charted between spatial definition and distinction and the 'common sense' – the occupational culture – of urban policing. The imagery of mapping is helpful here because as the contours of the Earth's surface are in flux around a basic stratified form, so the significance of particular sites – the social contours – move from back to foreground and are adjusted, yet always retain their fundamental semantic structure. The residual structures of chaos and control are closely related to the police force's search for coherent identity and rationale in an occupation which lacks a clear mandate of theory or practice. I want to stress once again that these attributions of significance cannot be falsified; if they were denied, the whole basis of urban policing by constables and sergeants would collapse.

Other identifications of space are less rigid, though each is related to the perspective of lower ranks. Home territories resonate with the values of secrecy and interdependency found among lower-ranked officers, hospitals with the low status of non-crime work. Sites of danger and trouble concern the action orientation and the hedonism as well as the protective secrecy of the police world.

It is possible to detect some of the features which Maureen Cain identified over a decade before I undertook my study of a different system of policing (and prior to the emphasis of police professionalism identified with contemporary policing). However, Cain's description and analysis has been extended and ordered to avoid the presentation of policing as a 'Flatland' by placing it within a framework of contoured relevancies (Rock, 1974). Within this basic spatial structuring of knowledge of the world, we find police officers constructing a culture designed to sustain their own ideas about and practice of urban policing.

5

The Manipulation of Time

You may ask PC 49 for the time. Though precise, his answer will conceal a complex network of ideas. The formal timetable at Hilton provides a framework within which the lower ranks construct and sustain a number of rather different 'clocks'. Like their knowledge of space and place, these alternative understandings are structured in terms of the relevancies of police work.

Three eight-hour shifts form the basis of the work timetable. These shifts – early morning, afternoon/evening and night – are interspersed with 'spare week', when officers work various hours before taking a long weekend leave that bridges an early and a night-duty shift. In many ways this formal timetable is similar to those of organizations that operate a system of continuous service or production, save that the product of the police can be less clearly defined.

At Hilton a number of specific police concepts are associated with this formal timetable. Police are expected to exhibit an awareness of time. As a recruitment pamphlet puts it, they have to 'take immediate action', 'observe and analyse' and 'interpret powers of arrest', which means that they must be vividly aware of their situation during work hours. *Time is now.* An awareness of the present is closely related to the sense of emergency which informs much police work. This heightens awareness of time and provokes speedy assessment of situations confronting officers. Of further relevance here is the fact that accuracy in recording events and in remembering them is important because *time is of evidential value.* The precise time at which officers arrive at an incident may be of vital importance when evidence of guilt is later evaluated in a courtroom. Therefore in police work, an assessment of the present may always be evaluated at a later date in a formal legal setting. Finally, *time is important because the office of constable is held continuously*. Although formally on and off duty at various times, every officer retains his powers of arrest and has to be constantly ready to exercise them. Police officers tend to see this feature of their work as distinguishing them off from 'civvies', a point which is emphasized when a constable deals with an inquiry from someone who wants to collect some property he has lost in the street.

> 'I'm sorry but your property is in the admin. They go home at 5 o'clock and they have the keys. . . . You see, we have civilians now who do this work for us. So we don't have the property at hand in the station office. The problem is they all go home at 5 o'clock and lock everything up, so we can't get to anything and that's where the system falls down.'

Time and authority

Although the system is exploited by PCs, supervisory officers require acceptance of the shift timetable as an indication of each officer's commitment to the ranked power structure of the force. The formal timetable represents 'management time' (Ditton, 1979; Thompson, 1967), against which the performance and loyalty of the work force can be assessed.

Lateness for duty therefore raises the issue not primarily of lost production or wages but of disrespect for the hierarchy of command. Some allowance is made for early turn – who does not find it difficult to get up at 4.30 a.m.? At other times lateness is of more serious concern.

> A constable is late for two days of night duty and a sergeant comments that he will 'sign his book' if it happens again. A constable reinforces the point: 'If you are late for two days running on early turn, you expect a bollocking from the skipper; he [the PC] has been late for two days, and if he got away with it, then anybody could.'

The association between time and authority permits supervisory officers to use time to control their subordinates – to encourage and reward no less than to discipline them. Reward can take the form of verification that a constable has worked for a longer period of overtime than is actually the case. Refusal to sanction overtime provides a means of disciplining a difficult officer. On one occasion a PC who is reckoned to be out to squeeze as much overtime as possible from his minimal work load arrests a person for causing criminal damage to some property. The inspector is cautious. The constable has suggested to his station officer that further inquiries should be made before the case goes to court. The arrest is made on Monday night; inquiries will apparently have to continue through Tuesday, which means that the suspect can appear before a court only on the following day, Wednesday.

The inspector overhears these comments. 'I suppose you are on weekly leave on Wednesday?'

PC: 'As a matter of fact, I am.'

Inspector: 'No, he can go to court on Tuesday, and you can do the inquiry tomorrow.'

The inspector is aware that the constable is able to claim double overtime, plus a further day off, if the court case is heard on Wednesday. The inspector comments later, 'You have got to watch – [names officer]; he will try that sort of trick very often. He won't put himself out unless there is something in it for him.'

This happens despite the fact that other officers who are not thought to be troublesome try the very same trick without comment or obstruction from supervisory staff.

This point about the sanction and restriction of overtime as a managerial ploy is reinforced when a new inspector joins the relief. The PCs are told that if they attend court after a tour of night duty, they can go home at about 4.00 a.m. and still claim the maximum amount of overtime due, as if they had worked the whole shift. A sergeant says that the discipline of the shift is being threatened: 'Where does it stop? I mean, once you start it, you don't know where it will stop, do you?' For him, alteration of 'management time' risks the breakdown of disciplinary control.

Work and non-work time

As far as Hilton's constables are concerned, real police work involves action – the sensation of speeding to an emergency call, time spent on crime, a fight or scuffle with a prisoner, ideally before making an arrest. When these events take place time passes quickly; work is being done; policemanship is being practised. 'Action' defines time. However, we know that policing is a rather slow, spasmodic type of work which is largely concerned with mundane incidents (Morris and Heal, 1981, pp. 5–13). The problem for the lower ranks is that this 'reality' of police work conflicts with their own view and, indeed, with their experience.

In fact, a police officer who merely stands on a corner, drives his vehicle along a road or patrols on foot with no particular destination in mind is involved in the task of policing – he is working. At Hilton, however, time spent like this is regarded as wasted; it is not work time.

> The driver of a Panda patrol radioed Hilton asking if there was any work to be done. The radio operator told him that nothing needed attention and he received the reply, 'Oh thanks, I'm bored. There's nothing to do.' A sergeant on duty as station officer heard this remark and went to his transmitter to instruct the officer, 'Well, do some police work then.'

Unless they experience 'action' the tension between the lower ranks' definition of policing and its actual conditions persists. As we shall see, officers handle the tension by structuring their timetable to maximize this central aspect of what they understand as real police work.

'Easing'

'Easing' (Cain, 1973, p. 37) fills the gaps between what officers consider to be work. It is recognized that certain periods of the day are supposed to be free from action, and easing in the station is permitted. A tea break is taken from about 6.00 a.m. to 6.30 a.m., and a lengthy night-duty break is scheduled for about 4.00 a.m.

On Sunday the PCs are allowed to stay in the station for long periods of time. A PC on my shift sometimes cooks Sunday breakfast, which occupies him and two colleagues for the duration of the whole shift. These are non-work times because it is thought that the chaotic and naive members of the public are safely off the streets.

Certain times of the year are also designated periods of official easing. At Christmas officers come to work but remain in the station throughout the eight hours of a shift on Christmas Day; some are allowed to go home early. Supervisors do not mind this because it gives them control over the constables, who are prevented from sneaking into a public house for a drink, going home unofficially and so on. Officers know that little work is expected of them around Christmas: 'It's nearly Christmas, so nobody is interested really; nobody wants to do any work, so it's a bit of a waste of time.' Easing is therefore non-work time during which you wait for action – real police work.

'Spare week' presents particular problems because officers are required to work, without a clearly formulated brief, between 8.00 a.m. and 4.00 p.m. on two days of the week. One of the PCs has named it 'BOFO (book on, fuck off) week'; there is no interest, no excitement in it. Aware of the difficulty, a sergeant once wondered how he could get the lads working, and he set up what he called a 'car squad'. During the two-day shifts of 'spare week' the squad patrolled in a police vehicle to find and remove cars parked in obstructive positions. Driving quickly, pitting yourself against a driver who might be rushing to get his vehicle away before you can remove it is fun; a consciousness of time is heightened; policing becomes action.

> The sergeant in charge of the squad came into the station and mentioned to a colleague, 'Oh, it's lovely out there, it's lovely out there. They're all running to their cars and driving off. It's lovely.'
>
> He was followed by a constable: 'I see how Traffic Division get a thrill out of this. It's great, isn't it? Its great fun having them removed. We must have got the chief £35 today – £7 a time. It's great.'

Of course, 'spare week' or any other time which appears to be quiet could be used in an entirely different manner – in building relationships with all manner of groups in the local community, for instance. However, work without action is non-work, and easing fills the gaps between bursts of activity.

Maximizing time

Although action and a heightened awareness of time are partly dependent upon the presence of people on the streets, officers at Hilton structure time to maximize a sense of speed, excitement and action (Horton, 1967). The slow and boring aspects of routine police work are speeded up into fast, action-oriented sequences of events by using the technology of unit beat policing, particularly cars and radios.

During tea breaks conversations about cars provide a constant source of interest; stories of police cars chasing other vehicles are commonplace. During patrol no opportunity is lost to speed time up by driving fast.

> The dog handler who works with our shift patrols in his purpose-built van. He is called to search insecure premises and arrives after a short period of time, stopping with a squeal of brakes. As he gets out of his vehicle he says to one of the PCs present, 'That made them get out of the way at – [a roundabout several miles away]. We were over there, you know, when we got your call. Not bad, eh?' He wears a wry smile on his face.

The roundabout is too far away for him to have covered the distance in the time; the banter reflects the enjoyment of a fast drive. So time is structured to accord with the values of the occupational culture, in particular the sustaining of action and excitement. After a fast and at times dangerous drive to an emergency call, the location of which was so far from us that it did not warrant our attention, I asked my colleague who was driving:

> 'The only reason you drove like that was because you wanted a fast drive?'
> He replied, 'Yes, well, it's a bit of fun, isn't it? It all makes for a bit of excitement and gets rid of a headache. It's all very exciting. And a fight is a good call, isn't it?

When coupled with personal radio communication, the use of vehicles· offers considerable opportunity to maximize excitement. If a radio message from the station sounds exciting – if it warns of a fight, for example – it can be passed to all officers with receivers in their vehicles. The tendency is to broadcast all calls which sound exciting and to call for assistance at the slightest hint of trouble. Speed and hedonism appeal to the officers, and emphasis is placed on the interdependency between them – the very feature of the police work group that Cain (1973) has documented. The technology of routine policing is reworked to create an experience which the officers define as typical and important.

Creating a sense of speed

Some periods of the day – between 3 a.m. and 6 a.m., for example – tend to be very quiet. During these times officers often create a sense of speed, mostly by using their vehicles and talking about car chases.

> I was patrolling with a colleague at about 3.00 a.m. when we saw the area car, driven by a member of our shift. The sergeant positioned his car behind and then in front of the other vehicle, encouraging a chase. The following twenty minutes were spent racing round the streets, the car at the head of the chase signalling left to turn right, driving on the wrong side of the road and so on.

Story-telling, joking and banter are typical and important aspects of life at a police station. At Hilton it is noticeable that stories are told at quiet times and are often associated with car chases or other incidents involving an element of action and excitement. Drama, elaboration and embellishment are used to transform narrative description of mundane events into a series of vignettes of significant moments which might confront the police officer at any time. Quiet and boring aspects of policing – non-work – are forgotten as a plethora of exciting tales are recounted to the relief.

A favourite time for stories is the 4 a.m. tea break, when the whole relief gathers in the station office.

On one occasion three stories of chases were told in succession. The first concerned a driver who sped away from a police vehicle; a long chase ensued until the offending vehicle crashed. When questioned, the driver said that the only reason he was trying to get away was that he thought he would be booked for speeding. This was followed by another officer who related a chase during which a bandit car attempted to get between a lamp post and the building line. A flash of sparks went up and the car carried on. He then continued with a further tale of a PC who used to be on his shift. He was sitting in his car when he heard a radio call involving a chase in another part of the city, some considerable distance from where he was. 'In ten minutes he was the second car in the chase, which was on 3 Division. Nobody can overtake Pete. The only time someone overtakes him is when he prangs it.'

Stories like these can be multiplied – but why are they so popular, and why are they told during quiet periods? When policing seems slow and dull and there is little action on the ground, stories stressing speed and action serve to remind officers of what they believe policing is really like. The past is transformed into a vivid present as a new sense of time is created and sustained.

Although it is not possible to assess the accuracy of accounts presented to the relief, there is a suggestion that officers elaborate a great deal.

The inspector in charge of the relief and a constable were involved in the arrest of a youth who had stolen a motor car. The inspector said, 'We got behind him and I thought we'd let him have a go. Sure enough, away he went. So we had a chase.'

The constable gave his account later, 'I told [the inspector] to stay behind him because he wanted to stop him and I said he might have a go, and he did. We got alongside and away he went. We chased him all the way down Low Corner and round until he stopped.'

Three months later these officers referred to the chase again, throwing doubt on their initial account. The inspector repeated the story to the whole relief – once more during the early hours of the morning when the relief had gathered to drink tea – and after he had completed it he added, 'It must have been the only chase where we slowed down to avoid overtaking him.'

Elaboration does not matter; accuracy is not central to the story. The important point is to heighten the sense of excitement and speed which is central to the occupational culture.

Slowing time down

A constable who wants to avoid reporting an incident will try to ensure that it has ended or another officer has arrived on the scene before he deals with it. The following request is broadcast over the personal radio system:

'John, could you go to outside the hospital where you'll meet Mr – who, according to the message we have got, says he has an accident report to make. Could you go along there? It's probably non-reportable anyway.'
'Yes, OK. Any transport?'
'If you walk he'll probably have gone by the time you get there.'
'True.'

Incidents like this one may also be accepted by PCs at times when they can be used to advantage. A constable who finds himself posted to an unsuitable meal break may take a call involving work and thus ensure that his break is changed to a later and preferred hour.

Time is slowed down in a more fundamental manner to control difficult suspects, especially when they are being questioned. Police have legal power to force their own definition of time on others; an arrest means that a suspect's time is wholly controlled by the police. When the car-removal squad speeds up its work, police control over people and time are closely related. Similarly, there are occasions when the legal control of police over suspects permits them to slow time down and, possibly, enhance their power.

Two men were arrested for a substantive offence but further evidence was required to secure their guilt. The officer who questioned them warned them, 'I tell you that you are going to stay here until you tell us who it was with you and broke the window with you.'

Similarly, another PC informed his station officer, 'I'll tell him [the suspect] that he's going to be kept here until he tells us the truth.'
    Sergeant: 'Well, he's going to be kept here anyway.'
    PC: 'I know, but I'll tell him that anyway.'

Techniques like these are also used outside the confines of the station. The threat that officers may return to a house at any time, unannounced and with the power to constrain people living on the premises, can strengthen police control. Two blacks and their female friends were once being questioned in a house where, it was believed, a person wanted on warrant was staying:

One of the men was asked, 'Come on, what's your date of birth? If you are not wanted, then you've got nothing to worry about. You give your date of birth.' The man said nothing, and after what must have been several minutes the officer said, 'Well, I can stand here all day waiting for your name and address. I want your date of birth first of all. What is it?' The man gave the information and a check was made over the personal radio. He was not a wanted man, and without comment the officers left the room for the stairs.
    One of the girls shouted, 'Well, don't come back, will you? He's not here.'
    PC: 'Yes, thanks very much. Yes, we'll come and see you again next week if you like.'
    We left the premises and the door was slammed behind us.

Time is slowed to the pace of the officer rather than that of the suspect; the legal powers of police are enhanced and secured.

Creating time: an economy of arrests

So far, the analysis of time had been concerned primarily with intrinsic aspects of police work. Most occupations are organized around intrinsic and extrinsic rewards, and, like the members of other occupations, policemen want to increase their wages as much as possible. Overtime provides an obvious source of extra money. It is good to 'feel a collar', and especially good if some overtime money can be made at the same time.

I arrived at Hilton for my first tour of duty, a night shift. A colleague met me in the station office, introduced himself and showed me to the charge book, where all records of persons arrested and charged are kept. He said, 'This is quite a good relief, really. You can see they do quite well. We have had lots of crime arrests this night duty.' On one of the few occasions when the officer in charge of Hilton sub-division wrote in the parade book, he told the constables that they had taken over half the total of crime arrests on the whole of the division during the past week. He went on: 'This is only done through hard work, and the staff are to be congratulated for their efforts.' These comments from supervisory officers indicate the assumptions that they tend to make about work time well spent. Constables know that whatever else they may do, arrests serve as one important indicator of competence and application. They can exploit such assumptions to increase their wages.

Incurring overtime means that it is possible to take time off at a later date or to ask for generous remuneration in lieu. During the period of my fieldwork the national economy was running at about 25 per cent inflation, which provided officers with an incentive to work overtime. If an officer arrests a suspect and attends court on his rest day, overtime is calculated at a higher rate than if he attends court on any other day. An extra day off in lieu is also granted.

After a week of night duty the whole relief has to take leave on Tuesday, which is especially unwelcome. After completing a late-turn shift on the Monday before this day off I record:

> The object of many PCs today is to get an arrest so that they can cancel their weekly leave – Tuesday – tomorrow. Sergeant – has already had his cancelled by Sergeant –, who has bailed a man arrested on Saturday to appear in court on Tuesday. This is contrary to force regulations. PC – is at coroner's court and – [another officer] has had his leave cancelled. A call came over the radio which sounded as if a suspect were illegally on premises. The car acknowledges

and – (who has already cancelled his leave) says to the crew of the car, 'Don't you go. You've already had your leave cancelled' – intimating that someone else should benefit from the arrest.

Just before the end of the shift on that same day, a sergeant and a PC arrest two men for gross indecency. Although it is not possible to infer that this arrest is made to ensure the cancellation of their weekly leave, a few days later I ask the constable about it.

SH: 'I don't know how you could stoop so low to arrest for gross on Monday. It wouldn't be because it was your weekly leave the following day, would it?'
PC: 'No, that's nothing to do with it, sarge. It's an offence against the Crown, and there's a power of arrest for it, and I simply arrested.
SH: 'I know – [the other officer involved in the arrest]. Who was the victim of the crime?'
PC: 'What?'
SH: 'Who was offended by the crime? There is no victim.'
PC: 'Well, I was. I was offended, and it is an offence.'
He smiles, and I say, 'I know better than that.'
PC: 'Yes, all right then.'
SH: 'Did they plead guilty?'
'No, remanded to a rest day.'

Two points arise from these data. First, time is structured to create and maximize overtime hours. Secondly, particular offences like 'gross' which take place at predictable times and places become 'good earners'.

The local football ground is another place where arrests can be made readily, particularly by the special squad of officers employed there. If juveniles are arrested, they are ejected from the ground; adults are charged and taken to court, usually providing overtime for an officer. The age of the offender can therefore make an arrest more or less lucrative.

I'm at court on Tuesday. I got old – and was chucking him out when I said, 'How old are you?'
He said, 'Seventeen.'
So I said, 'Right, you're nicked.' I have been waiting for

him to come seventeen for a long time. He's at court on Monday for another case, so I have to go to court on Tuesday.' This meant that extra overtime was incurred.

On another occasion I heard the following conversation at the local magistrates' court. The officer has been employed at the football ground:

'I hear that they're going to remand this lot. Ching! [Make noise of cash till.] The old money comes rolling in, doesn't it? I'm rest day today; I'm doing football tonight, so that means fourteen hours. Great!'
Another PC commented, 'All you think of is money. You're like the rest of us, you just think of the money. I'm getting a fair bit of overtime out of this as well.'

The national economy is certainly a factor in this economy of arrests. After the announcement of what many PCs considered to be an inadequate pay rise, one commented to a group of colleagues:

'Yes, I'll have to do a Smith now.' [PC Smith is an officer whose arrest work centres around the careful calculation of overtime.]
Another officer continued, 'Yes, I think that the villains had better watch out now. I've got to get rid of my overdraft, and my mortgage will be finished in one more year's pay. So I think the villains had better be watching out.'

Other officers do not use arrests to create time. They volunteer to attend an incident that requires a written report and runs over into an overtime period. One put it this way:

I have to get all the overtime I can. The wife is pregnant now, and that means £70 a month won't be coming in, so it's going to be pretty tight. I do all the 'footballs' I can, then if there is a sudden death going at about 2 o'clock, I try to get in on that and get a couple of hours' overtime out of it. The trouble is that it makes you tired, and some days you come to work feeling so tired that you are really irritable.'

There is no quota scheme of arrests at Hilton; among other values of the occupation, arrests mean overtime and increased wages. One sergeant remarks to a PC:

> 'If the population of – knew that policemen arrested be-
> cause of the card [overtime payment card], they would be
> shocked, wouldn't they?'
>   'Yes, it's terrible, really. I've made sixty hours out of this
> one already. Everything revolves around the card. It's like a
> cash register, really.

Two themes run as threads through this and the previous chapter. The first is that the police, particularly the lower ranks, exploit the freedom that they have within the formal organization of urban police work to mould the nature of policing so that it conforms with their image of it. Policing is defined as work which is full of action and fun: its primary activity is the making of an arrest. These aspects of their work are enhanced by the rank and file so that they can glean intrinsic satisfaction from urban policing and confer on it a certain significance. The formal timetable of the organization – 'management time', as it has been called – is manipulated to construct and sustain a particular view of police work.

This leads to the second point. In spite of policy changes, the occupational culture of lower ranks remains the residual stock of knowledge which informs their practice of policing. This much has now been demonstrated in the context of two of the most basic aspects of human experience, space and time (Schutz, 1974). The way in which the local population is perceived is no less closely related to police work.

6

The Police and the People

To an outsider a uniformed police officer symbolizes a certain measure of stability and security in the day-to-day world. Ease yourself into that uniform and, once the jacket is buttoned, the stability apparent to the outsider seems ambiguous. The intentions of people who call on you to deal with their problems are unclear – you do not know what they want or who they are; even the consequences of your own actions are less than certain.

To some extent we all have to deal with this problem: despite what some sociologists would have us believe, the world is an ambiguous place (Berger and Luckmann, 1967). Nevertheless, for the policeman ambiguity is a pressing concern. He looks around and sees people who are potentially disorderly; his own status and task, by contrast, carry the mask of authority. Police officers are not meant to be uncertain and ambiguous people.

Keep your jacket buttoned and join your colleagues because you will soon learn that policing – the notion of policing espoused by your rank-and-file colleagues – is based on a foundation which is firm and secure. The uncertainty of the neophyte has to be glossed over with certainty. Policing is straightforward and speedy work, the essence of which is prompt and resolute decision-making. Agonizing choices may underlie routine policing, but do not admit this to your colleagues – it is all a matter of straightforward common sense to them.

One means of coming to terms with the ambiguity facing you is to construct a map of the population that you police, complete with contours of space and time. This mental map is a compilation of your knowledge of the types of people with whom you can expect to deal, their likely responses, the events in which they may be involved, how they may frustrate or assist police activity (Bittner, 1967; Chatterton, 1975b; Manning, 1977; Rubinstein, 1973; Sacks, 1972; Skolnick, 1966). A sergeant describes the necessity of this mental map after he has faced the problem of moving from one police division to another with a very different population:

> It isn't like – [names another area], where you knew who you were dealing with. At – you are working in an upper-class area, and you don't know who you are dealing with. The rich expect far too much from you, and the weirdos, they expect a lot too. You really don't know who you are dealing with.

A probationary constable emphasizes the importance of knowing the population of his ground when he comments on the problem of stopping suspects in the street:

> At night times things are different. You are doing crime work then. I have done a few stops at night. Mind you, I don't agree with stopping everyone in sight – that's bad for the image of the police. My colleagues tell me that you get a nose for this sort of thing, but I haven't got that yet. There is an old boy who I stopped early on in my probation, and I suppose that every probationer has stopped him. He's just a bloke who likes to take a walk at night, and I know him quite well now.

These data link the officer's mental map of the population with time and, as we now see, with space:

> A new sergeant has recently joined Hilton, and I am driving him around the area. We pass a building nearing completion, and he asks its purpose. I explain that it is a new hall of residence for students at the local polytechnic. He asks, 'Do you get many left-wing activities up there, then?'
> We continue the patrol, and as we drive along a particular street, he asks, 'Is this the West Indian quarter, then?'
> SH: 'Not really. I think they probably mostly come from – ground. But they don't tend to live in any one part.'

Officer: 'Oh, I saw some shops back there which had West Indian names and oriental foods. I thought perhaps they lived around here.' (Later) 'I suppose you get a lot of trouble with the Irish. They move around and you can't trace them. What do you do with breathalysers?'

As these complex maps are learned, the ambiguity and uncertainty of policing are formalized as a series of workable typifications. Peter Manning (1977, p. 237) argues:

People are expected to fill categorical niches and fall into line with the commonsense police theory about human nature. The observed facts are assembled under the umbrella of a commonsense theory. The facts are not taken as a means to disconfirm the police theory of human nature.

Manning's remark boils down to the fact that PC 49 walks along Hilton High Street looking at the people around him in a very particular manner. We know that Hilton's officers view members of the public as if they were on the verge of chaos – this is their primary reason for policing the area. The police view is that humanity is fallen. People do not really understand the nature of their fellows; their gullibility, their lack of stability and common sense. The Hilton policeman's fear, unlike that of his American colleagues, is not of violence and danger but of disorder – quarrelling, 'messing about', the absence of proper guidelines for behaviour.

There are good grounds for this view – at least if you are PC 49. If people are on the edge of chaos, they need to be restrained, which may well require a range of techniques in police work that extends beyond the law. Further, given this view, PC 49's is superior to that of members of the public. They may be naive; he is not. His commonsense tells him how to evade the chaos that looms. There is a further twist to this; common sense is 'police common sense', which is not shared by the members of any other group and cannot be acquired by them – it belongs to policemen. PC 49 is not hoping to educate the public, he is preserving it from chaos. He subscribes to an attitude that brooks no appeal: 'We, the police, have a real knowledge; they, the public, do not and cannot have access to it.' Policing has its strangely gnostic aspect.

This, then, is the background against which more particular and flexible attitudes towards groups within the population are charted. At Hilton it seems that these groups are regarded in the light of their relevance to policing and the power structure of the local community. Key considerations are their actual or potential lack of control, the degree to which they may enhance the excitement and challenge of police work, their power to disrobe and demystify the occupational culture, particularly the secrecy and interdependency of that culture, and finally their power to call officers to account.

Blacks

Hilton has quite a large black British and West Indian population. During my first tour of duty at Hilton, a night shift, I ask my assistant station officer about them. He illustrates how blacks fit into the map of the population:

> There's quite a lot of feeling against blacks here. You wait till we come day duty, and you will see how many of them there are here. It's very difficult to deal with them because as soon as you talk to them, they accuse you of victimization. You get really annoyed sometimes, really boiled up, but you have to keep cool and not show it or they have got the better of you. It's very difficult like that here. . . . PCs around here don't like them. They always seem to campaign if anything happens. They go to the law centre down there. You see, there are people like – [names constable]; he says that he had no prejudice when he came here, but he has different ideas now. We had all those burglaries. They came from the hostel. . . . This week, last night, we had some, and you might remember that Sergeant – sent some PCs round there straight away, but they didn't go there.

Blacks are viewed negatively; they are usually described in derogatory terms – 'coon', 'nig-nog', 'spade', 'black', 'razor blade', 'nigger', 'wog', 'animal'. Of course, these terms are not derived solely from the police world; a clear connection exists between the police and the broader society (J. Clarke *et al.*, 1974; Institute of Race Relations, 1979). The generally negative attitude of Hilton's officers must be related to the position of black people within the power structure of British society. When discussing the possibility of a coloured constable's working at Hilton, an officer remarks: 'No, we don't want a "coonstable" here. Can you imagine? Half the relief would have to protect him if he went up the flats.'

An officer is selling his house, partly because he feels that he doesn't want to live next door to his black neighbour: 'You might call me a racist bastard and I know I haven't got a logical argument but I'm not going to live next door to them. . . . People on the other side of the road, racist bastards, are leaving their cars out the front of [the neighbour's] house and so on and are really trying to upset him. Well, I'm not racist. It's just that I think they're very nice people but I don't want to live next door to them. I know you can say that I'm wrong, but that's the way I feel.'

Generally, then, officers do not regard their ideas as any different from those of people who live near to them or in Hilton. This, however, tells us little about the more particular manner in which knowledge of blacks is moulded within police work.

Officers reckon that blacks do not like them; they tend to reciprocate that dislike. It is difficult to assess the hostility that black people might express towards the police if they were given an opportunity – it is in their interests to keep their feelings to themselves. However, on some occasions resentment does begin to surface. After being charged with an offence for which there is sound and credible evidence, a black youth tells the arresting officer, 'If you hadn't nicked me for that, you would have got me for something else.' A similar setting evokes a more general remark from a suspect who refers to the likelihood that a witness will testify for him: 'He's a white man. He won't help us. We're black.' The officer replies, 'If you don't shut up, I am going to get upset.' There is, then, general and reciprocal distrust, which is manifested in a number of ways.

Dislike and distrust are substantiated in the minds of Hilton's police by their suspicion of disorder, crime and a potential for violence among black people, particularly among youths (Cain, 1973, pp. 117–19). Blacks defy the primary occupational value of control. They cannot threaten to expose the actual practices of policing – they do not have power to do that – but they can and do challenge the police's claim to territorial control. As exemplars of a disorderly population, they provide continual evidence of the need for officers to employ their own particular remedies.

The precise extent of the involvement of blacks in Hilton's crime is not known; studies indicate that blacks are not disproportionately reflected in the official statistics of crime (Lambert, 1970; Stevens and Willis, 1979), and there is no apparent reason why this general finding should not be applied to Hilton. However, despite this evidence, officers at Hilton think the contrary to be the case, and blacks are under constant suspicion. While I am patrolling with an inspector during the early hours of the morning, we pass a black youth walking along the pavement. The inspector slows the car, saying: 'These coloured people certainly ask for trouble from us. They seem to hang about and look suspicious.' He believes this, despite the fact that white youths in the same setting are of interest; they, however, draw no comment. Other officers blame blacks for a good deal of the peacekeeping work in which they are involved:

> A constable argues: 'It's the blacks around here who cause most of the trouble with disputes and things. You can almost bet that on a Sunday afternoon you'll be called to a domestic dispute of some sort. If we didn't have these disputes, then there'd be very little to do around here, I reckon.'

Another common assumption that officers make is that blacks (again, particularly black youths) tend regularly to be involved in crime. Commenting in a general manner, the constable quoted above mentions the colleague who 'had no prejudice when he came here' but now has 'different ideas'. This latter PC is standing in the station yard when he hears shouting in the cells:

> He asks: 'Is it a drunk?'
> Colleague: 'No, five for GBH.'
> Officer: 'A coon?'
> Colleague: 'No, Irish.'

His assumption is that blacks commit violent crime. A supervisory officer expresses this same view after attending a club where a large number of black people congregate. A police officer has been assaulted outside the club, and several officers from Hilton attend the incident. When they return to the station the supervisor comments: 'Mind you, the reason we need dogs for the coloureds is because they're so bloody violent, and that's why you want them.' Opinions sometimes take an even more extreme form. One officer suggests that instead of embarking on the small social studies project on an aspect of their subdivision that probationary constables usually undertake, 'I could write a thesis. Exterminate all the niggers and you wouldn't have any problem. Just exterminate all the niggers.' This view is indicative of the general suspicion of black people and assumptions about their involvement in crime, their potential for violent behaviour and their resistance to control. After a colleague fails to investigate an allegation of assault with sufficient care, the officer dealing with the case comments, 'Well, sarge, it's not really for me to legislate. They were a couple of coons shouting at each other, and it's difficult in those circumstances, I suppose.'

Finally, blacks are thought to be able to exploit their feelings about the police by drawing on the assistance of the local law centre and then threatening police security. A community worker at a hostel for homeless youths offers similar help, and criticism is directed at him for his activities. A sergeant expresses the general view of the station when he is asked by the clerk of the local magistrates' court what he thinks of the hostel.

Officer: 'Well I know – [the person who runs it] very well, and I find him OK, but when you are arguing with him he is only willing to go so far. It's like an extreme political argument or a religious one. You can't go any further. Mind you, it's a Fagin's kitchen down there. We had a juvenile in from there the other week, and we cleared up half our crime book with the breakings he had done.'

Clerk: 'Yes, but he has a point of view to put across. He is very helpful to us down here and will stand bail and get the boys to court. . . .'

Officer: 'Yes, I know that and he is perhaps coming round to our way of thinking.'

It is interesting that the sergeant thinks the community worker has changed his views by getting boys to court and by ensuring that they keep bail. The community worker has apparently accepted the police view, leaving the police perspective of distrust intact. A similar point is made by other evidence. An inspector makes some comments about a police community liaison officer who has given evidence of character for a black youth charged with robbery.

> This is what I mean when I say that some have gone over to the other side. We should not treat anybody, be they black or white, with preference. If we do, then we get away from the idea of equality for all and the police giving equal treatment to both black and white. And we can't allow them to say that they are arrested just because they are black. If we allow that, then we forget that the law has to be upheld and the respect it deserves given to it. If anyone fails to give a lack of respect or breaks the law, he must be arrested.'

It is certainly unusual for a police officer to give positive evidence of character in mitigation; no judgement is made of this action. Despite the novelty of the case, these data are further indication that typifications of blacks are not fundamentally altered by any extraordinary event, whatever credibility the event might have. Modification of the accepted police view is understood as 'going over to the other side'. As Manning (1977) argues: 'The facts are not taken as a means to disconfirm the police theory of human nature' (p. 237).

These, then, are the attributed characteristics that tend to mould the typification of blacks: their dislike of the police; their presumed disorderliness and predisposition to crime; their violence; and their exploitation of their grievances by drawing on the facilities of the law centre, Community House and, as the data above suggest, some community relations officers. The view is certainly a negative one; it is prejudiced and deeply rooted in the officers' assumptions about their work.

A small amount of data also indicates the relevance of this typification to the occupational culture of urban policing. Control having been established as central to that culture, the truculence attributed to blacks justifies the perceived necessity for continued vigilance and the use of all the available sub-cultural techniques of routine policing. Further, because this attitude is overwhelmingly negative, it also provides opportunities for challenge, police activity and therefore enjoyment, a point illustrated by my record of the following incident:

> A youth club catering for blacks had recently opened in the subdivision. On two evenings each week it catered for these people, and despite the large number of youths attending, there was very little need for police supervision. One particular night, a Friday, the night-duty shift was drinking tea, and a probationer constable mentioned that he thought the club should be supervised. At that stage I walked into the 'tea room'. The inspector said, 'Right, we'll go down there tonight and turn a few of them over; if they are shouting and mucking about, we will nick a few.'
>
> A sergeant who had been out of the room entered, and one of the PCs said to him, 'We've got permission to beat niggers tonight, sarge; have a few tonight, sarge.'
> [In the event, other duties prevented the officers from going to the club.]

A dislike and distrust of blacks is certainly evident from this episode, but even more it indicates the pleasure afforded by a scuffle or fight – by action. Indeed, it seems that the typifications of the occupational culture are categories by which information is moulded. The occupational culture is a shared series of ideas which both sustain and are sustained by the cognitive map that we have documented.

'Challengers'

'Challengers' are those who have the power, in principle, to question the assumption that Hilton's police retain sole control over persons held in custody and over other areas of police work. These challengers are in a position to pierce the secrecy and protection of the lower ranks. They comprise two groups in general: lawyers and doctors. A third group, social workers, is less important in this respect but nevertheless may question police action.

Lawyers

Lawyers are a particular threat because they can unmask police practice and can articulate the grievances of their less authoritative and less coherent clients. When it seems likely that a lawyer will be involved after an arrest, officers have to 'cover themselves' in case a complaint arises. An inspector in charge of a relief is especially aware of this problem:

> There are some people who you would get a solicitor for and make entries in the daily record book because you know that they would complain against you. There are others you would not bother with. Each case has to be dealt with on its own, and you need experience to know what to do.

So is another officer:

> He had arrested two persons suspected of overstaying their residence in this country went to the canteen to purchase a meal for his prisoners. One of the detainees was requesting the presence of his solicitor, a request the officer did not want to grant.
>   He was asked why he was buying the food – 'You're going to get him a meal? You must be getting soft. You must be cracking up.'
>   Officer: 'I'm backing it both ways. It may be that his landing conditions are OK, so I'm backing it both ways.'

The meal is presumably a tactic gleaned from the experience to which the inspector refers, as is an assessment of whether or not the person held in custody is likely to cause trouble by making a complaint.
    Another inspector is also aware of the likelihood of a complaint (a 'one-docket') when he says to two detectives who have arrested some suspects for attempted burglary:

> I hope you have checked to see who his solicitor is. Is it an MP? We'll be getting a one-docket from the House of Commons.

Other officers are somewhat less discreet.

> A number of suspects charged with a serious assault are in the cells. A supervisor goes to check their condition, and when one of the prisoners shouts through the wicket gate he is punched.
>
> Prisoner: 'I want my solicitor.'
> Officer: 'You don't get anything.'

The nature of this suspect's alleged offence undoubtedly influences the officer's response; the request for a solicitor is a further and probably more important stimulus.

Despite legal provisions, this attitude towards solicitors militates against a suspect's being able to seek advice while he is being held in custody. An investigating officer expresses a broadly shared view when he talks about a suspect's request for a solicitor.

> That one really got up my nose. He was within an ace of getting his head slammed up against the wall. Who the fucking hell does he think we are? 'I want my solicitor.' He'll want us to get the fucking law centre down here soon. They make me fucking sick.

Officers clearly do not like solicitors, and particularly when they act as 'mouthpieces' for clients. This is one of the reasons why the law centre is regarded as a troublesome place. Two black youths have been arrested for obstructing the highway. They plead not guilty and are represented at the magistrates' court hearing. The arresting officer says:

> 'If it was you or I, we wouldn't be represented. It's amazing how they get represented.'
>
> Before a case at the Crown Court is heard the arresting officer comments, ' – [the suspect] is on legal aid, isn't he?'
> 'Yes, he got it through the law centre. All right, isn't it?'
> 'Oh, crooks anonymous.'

Solicitors from the law centre are therefore contaminated by the criminality and disorderliness of their clients, which makes police work all the more difficult and policemen all the more wary.

This lack of trust, which is fuelled by the idea that the solicitor is little more than a misinformed puppet, helps to create and sustain the view that the courtroom hearing is like a game – one not wholly disliked by some officers (Carlen, 1976):

> Officer: 'Were you questioned very rigorously?'
> Colleague: 'No, not rigorously but aggressively. I thought the barrister was a bit obvious. He said it was all fabrication.'

To be 'a bit obvious' is to overplay. Two officers comment on another lawyer's performance, 'You'd have thought that he was trying a murder charge, wouldn't you, not a breach of the peace.'

The stipendiary magistrates before whom suspects sometimes appear can also be 'challengers'. PCs come to know the preferences of their magistrates and present cases accordingly. Taking a 'dodgy job' to a 'foreign' court risks unmasking.

> Two of Hilton's officers had arrested suspects for attempting to take a motor vehicle. Their colleagues discussed the arresting officers' unwillingness to construct the evidence in order to gain a conviction: 'And it is a foreign court anyway, so there were are. You see, he doesn't believe in that sort of thing.'

But although officers hold certain negative views, they also enjoy the challenge that the courtroom offers.

> A constable is telling two sergeants of a performance in court when he disarmed a lawyer by asking, 'If I may refer to my original notes?'
> The sergeant replied, 'You ought to be an actor. You are in the wrong job.'
> Constable: 'You are dead right. That's what it is. That's what it's all about.'
> Other sergeant: 'That's it, that's our stage. That's what it's all about. You've got to be a good actor.'

The challenge of a lawyer can legitimately be made in court – the rules of that game are known. However, the rules that are acknowledged when suspects are questioned do not encompass intervention by a lawyer.

Doctors

Doctors are thought to have a similar capacity for unmasking police work. When doctors at the local hospital ask why a number of injured persons have been referred to them from Hilton police station, officers say, 'The hospital is very "anti" at the moment with [a suspect] being beaten up.' Another officer who comments on the same incident makes this point:

> the hospital took photographs of him, you know, not the defence. The doctor measured every single cut on his face and put it on a picture of the face and they took photographs – not the defence.

The risks in cases like these are obvious. However, doctors meet less opposition than do defending lawyers – they can help the police by checking the health of a suspect and by taking responsibility should it deteriorate. Tension arises when they step beyond the bounds of what officers consider to be purely medical duties to make judgements about police action. It is then that doctors become 'challengers'.

> A boy has been taken to the paediatric section of a local hospital because it is alleged that his father has beaten him. A doctor asks the inspector dealing with the matter, 'If the police take initial action on these things, then I understand that it becomes a police case and that is something which is not often liked because if it's shown to be a mistake, not the fault of the parent of the child who's suffered injury, there is unnecessary stigma.'
>
> Inspector: 'No, I don't think that's the case at all. We aren't big ogres, you know. We were doing social work before the social services ever began, and we're quite capable of doing it, and we're quite capable of using our discretion in the matter. I don't think there's any stigma in going to court now in this day and age. . . .'
>
> The doctor listens and says that he is only seeking information, not opinion.

Many complex reactions may have provoked the inspector's response. One point that emerges from this incident is the police view that they have the right to control their own affairs, with which doctors should not attempt to interfere. It is the capacity of doctors to challenge police work that issues in the protection of autonomy.

Social workers

A similar claim to privacy and autonomy frames the manner in which social workers are understood. On the one hand, social workers are thought to affect police action by default. They are rarely available when the police require them and, when they are available, often unco-operative. As one sergeant put it:

> Fucking social workers. They never deem anybody and you can never get hold of them anyway because all the nutters we get are outside office hours. So they never do anything.

Another officer said on one occasion:

> I should think that Social Services up there have just about had enough of her because they [the police] phoned up a social worker, and for one of them to get up in the morning is quite something. I don't think he realized there are two 2 o'clocks in the day.

On the other hand, social workers are thought to be ignorant of the conditions in which police work is performed; they do not understand human nature. When an officer remarks on the motivation of a suspect, the reaction of a colleague illustrates this point:

> 'I feel sorry for him. He's not a villain. He doesn't do thieving out of villainy. He just doesn't know why he's done it.'
>   Other officer: 'Blimey, we've got a social worker here.'

Two home beat officers discuss the bad housing conditions found in the subdivision. A constable who has been listening says, 'Bloody social workers.' With these feelings in mind, an officer expresses pleasure when during a court case a social worker suggests that a punitive sentence might be suited to his client. This view contrasts with a police perspective on decision-making:

> Social workers introduce a lot of greys into the situation.
> Years ago things used to be black or white and you knew
> where you stood. Now there's lots of grey and you don't
> know where you are. I think we ought to get back to being
> policemen. I mean, look at home beat men. They are sup-
> posed to be social workers and not policemen.

Social workers do not share the basic assumptions underpinning 'police common sense'. However, they can sometimes
make decisions about individuals in whom the police also have
an interest and in this way challenge police work.

'Disarmers'

'Disarmers' are members of groups who can weaken or neutralize
police work. To the police a disarmer has an uncertain status.
Although it is sometimes necessary to take action against disarmers, officers have to temper that action carefully. The frailty,
age and/or sex of these people may prompt the sympathy and
criticism of others monitoring police work.

Women

Police ideas about women cannot be isolated from broader social
trends. Women are reckoned to be frailer than men, so in certain
contexts they can soften or neutralize police values and action
relevant to men. It is noticeable that when in custody women are
not subject to rigorous control. Criticism of a local store detective who prosecutes a large number of women for stealing items
of small value is prompted quite simply by the objection that
these women may not be guilty.

Whatever their offence, women held in custody are likely to be
afforded 'soft' treatment:

> A young woman is arrested for theft, and it is also found that
> she is wanted for questioning by the Special Branch. The
> station officer allows her to sit in his chair at the charge

room desk, and when he wants to use it he asks a constable to get her another. This is done despite the fact that the girl is of black British origin, a suspected thief and political activist.

A woman is arrested for criminal damage. She is exceedingly abusive and unco-operative towards the arresting officer but, nevertheless, he remains calm. He brings a cup of tea to the charge room and places it on the desk at which she is sitting. The woman knocks it off the desk. 'Look, love, don't be stupid. I was going to enjoy that cup of tea.' He gets another cup and the same thing happens. He remains calm.

Although precisely matching data involving men are not available, there is sufficient evidence to support the contention that if a man had knocked that tea over, he would have met with a rather different reaction. Further, if a man sat in the station officer's chair, he would be ordered to sit on the bench provided in the charge room or placed in a detention room.

Of course, there are occasions when women resist arrest and force has to be used, but even then restraint is exercised:

A supervisory officer arrests a woman who obstructed him while he administered a breath test to her male companion. After she had been brought to the station and charged, he tells a group of officers: 'It's a good job she's a woman. I haven't been nearer hitting a woman for years. If it hadn't been a woman, it would have been assault on the police and Sergeant – would have been making an entry in the daily record book.'

There is even a serious suggestion from a constable that women should not normally be prosecuted for motoring offences:

After a constable had reported a woman, a colleague asked, 'You haven't reported a woman, have you? That's a bit strong, isn't it?'
'It was dangerous turning against the sign at that bloody junction.'
Other constables join in the questioning.

Ideas about the physical weakness, dependence and culpability of women which are current in our society lie behind these remarks. Their sexuality also plays some part because it is believed to be easy for them to allege that an officer has made sexual advances. A very small number of women who live at Hilton alert officers to this danger. One woman prompts the comment: 'Most PCs won't go there on their own because she usually appears at the door in a frilly nightie.' Many of the terms used to describe women carry sexual connotations – 'slag', 'nigger bait', 'tart' – and we have seen (p. 40) that a woman who alleges that she has had sex with police officers is marked out as dangerous. Women therefore provoke a certain ambivalence among officers – they can 'disarm' police action.

Children

The other group that can disarm the police is children. Hilton is a poor area; children play in the streets and are very obvious to patrolling officers. Some officers blame parents for their children's behaviour:

It's living around here and growing up in a bad family.

The way parents treat the kids round here is criminal, yes, criminal. My kids would never be allowed out on their own at that age, never.

Some people say that the parents can't control the kids. I don't know, I think they can.

The question is: how much blame can be attributed to a child who offends? And, equally important, how much blame will be attached to him by courts and others who deal with children after officers have carried out their own work?

Further, officers wonder if their action with children will be backed by senior officers and the juvenile court. The 'soft' handling of children that is advocated adds to officers' frustrations. An officer refers to the juvenile bureau scheme and its disarming effects: 'If you are dealing with a leary and insolent young brat, do you put that down as information?' Although the officer does not work at Hilton, his remark reflects the situation there. In the station and, more generally, as a part of the local population, children can raise questions about the appropriateness of police action.

This does not always prevent policemen from using a certain amount of force on children who commit offences. They may be given 'one slap around the left ear' or 'a thick ear'. But such force differs from that used on adults, and the reason for this is the disarming characteristics of children, even though some officers believe children are becoming more crafty:

'They know all the tricks of the trade. You've got fourteen-year-olds coming in here who know all the tricks before you get them in.'
    'Yes, they're trying to outwit you more. They're getting much more subtle.'

Subtlety is all the more serious for Hilton's officers when the disarming qualities of children is taken into account. Along with women offenders, children make officers feel uncertain. The police know how they would like to deal with them but fear the consequences of exposure.

The mental map of the population which has been described is detailed in terms of primary and secondary social contours. The underlying reality of a disorderly public is fundamental and unchanging: the secondary contours of 'blacks', 'disarmers' and so on are more flexible, moulded to context with greater precision. It would be misleading to suggest that all officers regard lawyers, women and so on in the same way. What we have here are the dominant groups of Hilton's population, with which various kinds of policemanship are associated. Further, there is a gap between attitude and action which complicates the picture: individuals can move from one category to another; other less central groups are also of relevance. Nevertheless, if you put on that blue serge uniform and join Hilton's officers, the attitudes illustrated above are the ones you will hear expressed in the conversation of station staff. You will not be prevented from holding other opinions, but they will have to be pitted against the dominant views expressed here.

In part, all of the secondary views (those of 'challengers' and others) have to be understood in the context of the power structure of the local community and of Britain itself. Blacks encounter prejudice partly because of their position within British society. The very negative and suspicious attitude towards black youths is firmly lodged in the stock of knowledge that directs officers' work and has a clear link with these broader societal structures of power and inequality (James, 1979; Reiner, 1981). However, the views of the police form not a straightjacket but a framework within which particular cases are worked out. The assumptions about blacks, 'challengers' and 'disarmers' constitute the commonsense of policing.

Although this mental map of the population is based on our social structure, it also reflects to some extent the values and practices of the lower ranks. 'Challengers' can offer a threat to the secrecy and interdependence of policing; for some officers they can also precipitate a stimulating game in court. Blacks provide for action, control and excitement. Policing is sustained by such stimuli; they create *and* maintain a very particular perspective, since distance is maintained between the police and the community policed – and this distance has to be assured if the fundamental map of the population outlined in this chapter is to remain intact.

7

Suspects and Strategies

The 'prisoner' binds together central elements of the occupational culture. 'Prisoner' or 'body' are not just names given to someone who is taken into custody for a criminal offence; the terms also cover the range of those charged with public order offences. Making an arrest can offer the experiences of action, challenge and, most important, control; arresting a prisoner, 'getting bodies', is the primary act of good policing, though it is a minor one in terms of the total amount of police work (Morris and Heal, 1981, pp. 9-13). Some prisoners are more prestigious than others:

> A constable makes great play of an arrest he has made: 'I had to arrest somebody yesterday, you know.'
> Sergeant: 'A juvenile?'
> PC: 'No.'
> PS: 'Old-age pensioner?'
> PC: 'No.'
> PS: 'Female shoplifter?'
> PC: 'No.'
> PS: 'Drunk?'
> PC: 'No. Pecuniary advantage, actually.' The constable redresses the balance by asserting the control he exhibited: 'We got into the station and he called me "son". I had to teach him the error of his ways.'

Whatever his status might be, the challenge that a 'prisoner' makes to police control, the visible evidence of disorder that he proffers, serves as verification of the conviction that the whole population is potentially, and in parts actually, in a state of disorder. A 'crime arrest' is interpreted as *the act* that keeps chaos at bay, a view fuelled by the centrality of the figures for arrest and charge, the major measure of police performance. Support is therefore continually given to the police view of 'prisoners' as representatives of a pervasive type within the general public. If you want to be a police officer, you will have to get used to taking notice of the figures.

Figures

Prisoners are bodies that can be counted. They are an easy and readily identifiable measure of work which is always at hand (Chatterton, 1975b; Bottomley and Coleman, 1980). When I arrived for my first tour of duty at Hilton a colleague emphasized to me the number of charges taken during the current administrative year.

> After returning to work from fourteen days' holiday, a colleague told me, 'You are station officer for most of this week. We took a right hammering over the last fortnight; we have really put a lot of bodies in the charge book. A lot of grief, but you can see we're on 2,100 charges. Pretty good really. We've been really busy.'

Drunks add to the charge figures, and therefore to the rating of the station, but there is some doubt about their pertinence:

> The same sergeant was talking to a junior CID officer: 'They took ten charges last night, so they must have been pretty busy.'
> CID: 'Well, I suppose they were drunks.'
> Sergeant: 'No, there was some drugs in it as well. We're up to 2,300 charges already.'
> CID: 'That's busy, is it?'
> Sergeant: 'Yes.'

Probationer constables have to submit to their supervisory sergeant the number of arrests that they make each month. No quota of arrests exists, but if an officer is short on his figures, he may well ask to be employed on the van patrol during night duty, which will offer him an opportunity to make some arrests fairly quickly.

PCs employed on specialist squads are even more aware of 'keeping their figures up' (James, 1979). A constable who has been recently seconded to work on a squad established to combat a large number of car thefts makes this clear when I ask him if he has enjoyed working on the squad:

> Yes, you have got a lot more freedom when you are doing that. But it is not like beat crimes, where you have a bit of a lazy time because you have got a diary to fill in and you have got to justify yourself. There is only one way to do that. That is to get out and do stops and to nick people.

Similarly, the crew of the plain-clothes patrol car constantly watches the numbers of stops and arrests it makes, aware of the importance of this measure of performance.

Figures, then, are a ready-made, primary measure of competent policemanship. They are sufficiently important to extend beyond comparisons between individuals and groups to those between Hilton and other stations:

> ' – [another ground] not as busy as this place, not on figures anyway.'
>
> 'I was station officer at – last night. We're 200 up on their charge book already this year and about a hundred up on breathalysers.'
>
> SH: 'Yes, it is pretty quiet down there really.'
>
> Officer: 'No, they had more charges than us last year but this year it is different.'

These comparisons between stations are fostered even if force regulations are bent to raise the figures, which is what happens when an arrest is made by Hilton officers in the neighbouring section of Bluecoat, where the 'prisoners' should have been taken.

> After the arrest of two youths, the following conversation took place over the personal radio system. The driver of the police vehicle said, 'Two bodies coming to Hilton.'

A CID constable intervened: 'They nicked it from Hall Road, so they might as well go to Bluecoat. Then it's a straight red-inker [arrest recorded].'

A Hilton PC interjects, 'If they come to Hilton, we can both have one.'

Sergeants and inspectors do not mind the extra work involved when 'prisoners' come to Hilton from other sections because they know that their PCs expect support, and the governors are pleased if the figures are kept up. Crime figures are certainly dear to the heart of the officer in charge of the station – he congratulates his officers for their efforts and writes a tribute in the parade book. A former incumbent had made rather similar comments:

It has not gone unnoticed that over the past two or three weeks a lot of good work has been put in by a lot of officers in the field of crime. Many good arrests have resulted, and obviously this gives me cause for great pleasure. The officers concerned are to be congratulated on their efforts, and I know that they will continue, as there are many more wrongdoers who have yet to be brought in; Mr – – (the officer in charge of the CID) is also appreciative of the efforts made and wishes to be associated with my remarks.

Senior officers know that references to 'figures' touch a central nerve of the occupational culture and provide an opportunity to motivate lower ranks; the status and competence of their stations are certainly enhanced by them. They also know that if they use the figures for reported crime to illustrate the considerable disorder in their subdivision, an impression of the monumental task that they face is publicly sustained. However, no matter how low the figures of arrest may be, they demonstrate that the officers are battling against the problem and will continue to do so if the manpower strength of the station is maintained. Figures have this double-edged significance for senior officers. In one go they confirm the failures and successes of police work.

Although it has not been possible to obtain clear data on this point, during the course of a discussion about crime figures with an officer in charge of a neighbouring station, a similar explanation is given. I point out that one of the senior officers of the force is arguing that the peacekeeping work of policing is of great importance and should be considered in conjunction with crime control. He replies:

> Well, he [the senior officer in question] has never been a working policeman in this force and it might be all right to say these things in – [names previous city force of senior officer], where the pressure is not on, but it is quite another thing here. Anyway, he is not really helping things. You see, the reason I worry about the charge figures at this station is because if they drop, we get less men allotted to us next year, so I try to keep them up. This is the Chief Officer's policy, so you see how – makes us do this sort of thing. He is in it as much as anyone.

Clearly, for this senior officer and, presumably, for others, the development of an adequate measure of performance is a dilemma mediated by the chief officers of the force. Figures of arrest and charge become a thread that runs through all levels of policing; the butt end of this thread remains with the constable on the street. For him figures forge and strengthen the idea that policing is indeed concerned with the chaos implicit in the nature of things. Yet, strangely, at one and the same time this tangible measure enhances both the police conviction that disorder is rife and confidence that the police are able to counter the chaotic drift that the figures represent.

'Prisoners'

The choice of the word 'prisoner' to describe an arrested person who is held in custody is significant. Why not 'suspect', 'detainee' or some other word? The underlying police assumption is that, like a prisoner held in gaol after conviction and sentence, a person in police custody requires a measure of control. Further, it suggests that the police assume a suspect's guilt. The other frequently used term, 'body', suggests detachment and indicates the appropriateness of behaviour that tends to deny, or at best to ignore, the motivation and humanity that a detained person might reveal. Incidents have been cited that illustrate the need of some 'prisoners' to assent to constraints which exceed proper legal directives, to acquiesce to the personal authority of the officers dealing with a charge. In the light of the fact that certain suspects can disarm routine practices, the initial assumption is made that they should all speak when spoken to, stand up and sit down as ordered and generally submit to the directions of the officers in the case. If submission is not forthcoming, some redress is required by the police. When a suspect attempts to escape from custody one day and is recaptured, the sergeant on duty at the time recalls:

> I was station officer and had to stand between the prisoner and my relief. When he was captured they all wanted to kick his bollocks off (and that was my relief, I might add). They were like a pack of animals wanting to get at him.

Even when a station officer is sympathetic towards a suspect, the rule of control remains. Here it is invoked when a sergeant disagrees with the need to arrest for a drugs offence;

> A squatter has been arrested by two CID constables and a uniformed PC for possession of a controlled drug. A minute trace of an unknown substance in a used syringe is involved. The sergeant turns to the officers, in the presence of the prisoner, and says, 'What's all this shit? You're not interested in that.'
>
> One of the detectives replies, 'No, I'm not interested in it at all, but it was found there and we have to find out what is going on.'
>
> Another constable says that he will complete the administration of the charge.
>
> The sergeant looks at them in disgust and begins to leave the charge room when the prisoner says to him, 'Now, you're surely not going to do me for that? I'm trying to get off the stuff, and you won't help me at all if you do me for that. It's as offensive to me as it is to you.'
>
> Sergeant: 'I don't know what I'm going to do, but I'll make my own mind up, thank you.'

Suspects are regarded as property which is under the control of the arresting and station officer.

Two constables arrest some youths for suspected rape. One of the officers describes the arrest: 'I found them and put them in the back of my Panda, then – [another officer] comes up, leaps out of his Panda and gets in the passenger seat of mine. He turns round to them and says, "I'm arresting you for rape." That was it. He wasn't anywhere near.'

Later, after the youths have been questioned, the officers redistribute their property: 'Right, decision time. Who takes what?' The officer making the initial arrest says, 'I take the rapist and you take the other one.'

This view of suspects as property also means that an arresting officer should know what is happening to his 'prisoner' while he is held in the station. If physical force is used, the arresting officer may have to give evidence to a court and must be ready to answer any allegations made against him. Being property, a suspect should therefore not be questioned without the knowledge or permission of the arresting officer – that is, his 'owner'.

Two men have been arrested for a substantive and are suspected of further offences. The station officer asks a constable to assist in what seems to have become violent questioning, but before it begins he ensures that the arresting officer is present: 'I think – [the officer arresting] should be with you when you question the prisoner.' In fact, although the arresting officer takes his colleague to the cell where the questioning is to take place, he does not remain there during the interrogation, and this is the subject of comment by another constable. 'Old – didn't half hit the prisoner yesterday. [The arresting officer] was in the canteen while – was thumping his prisoner.'

If a suspect is held at Hilton, waiting for officers from another station to collect him and take him to the area where his offence has been committed, he is considered the property of that collecting officer. One of our PCs has talked to a prisoner who does not belong to him and thinks he may be able to elicit some useful evidence by further questioning, but he also realizes that he is not dealing with his own property:

I wish it was our job because I reckon, given an hour or so, I could work the oracle on him. His bottom lip is trembling, and he's got something to hide. I just wish it was our job, so I could do a little bit of investigation on it.

Police assumptions like those about control and property create a context within which submission to police authority tends to be more important than invoking the legal rules concerned with detention and questioning. Rules like Judges' Rules are irrelevant (Home Office, 1977) and, indeed, can be a source of amusement rather than part of a serious procedure. Two transport police officers bring a suspect to Hilton, and the station officer comments: 'Right couple of lawyers we have got out there. They are trying to decide who cautioned him before he was arrested. . . .' Again, the understanding of police work that dominates the handling of suspects is that of the lower ranks. They mould force policy into workable strategies in order both to deal with the problems of their work as they define them and to sustain their own culture.

Strategies of control

Very little is known about how police officers actually exercise their authority other than in formal, legalistic ways. It is often claimed that laws and rules are moulded within strategies and tactics which are meaningful to the lower ranks, but empirical evidence to back the assertion is rare (Manning and Van Maanen, 1978, pp. 238–55). Strategies of control are the techniques employed regularly by Hilton's officers in encounters with people who may have committed an offence; tactics are the adjustment of strategies to meet particular contexts of police work (Silverman, 1970, p. 186). How does a police officer use this wide range of strategies to cajole, prompt, advise and force people – to him, disorderly people – into doing what he requires? In less academic terms, if chummy doesn't behave, what do you do?

Older officers tend to take the view that their younger colleagues have lost a lot of the finesse that they themselves possessed in their own day (Punch, 1979b, p. 49). Some of the home beat officers, whose specialist work could broadly be called 'community relations', feel that the aggressive approach of younger officers leaves much to be desired. Two of them discuss the issue and conclude that the ineffective juvenile court system and unit beat policing are root causes:

'I can tell you, I hear more young men around this station talking about summary justice than I've ever done.'

'Yes, I agree with you, but more and more young men here are hitting people, because they don't think it's worth doing them at court.'

Later in the discussion: 'Yes, you're dead right, that's another old chestnut. The blokes here just don't know how to walk a beat. They never get out and meet anybody. They don't know how to talk to anybody. I think it's terrible. There is a proper way to walk a beat, you know. There's a proper way to do it, but do they know? No, they don't. They want to ride around in Panda cars, and they don't want to get out and walk around, meet people and talk to people. They just haven't got a clue.'

Following an incident during which a PC hit a coloured youth with his truncheon, a telephonist who had worked at Hilton for a considerable number of years made the following comments:

Since the old personal radio [PR] came in, I think that instead of talking their way out of trouble like the old coppers did and getting by that way, they just pull their truncheons out and shout for assistance on the PR. They don't talk their way out of it at all. They just ask for assistance and get their truncheons out.

Remember that the telephonist and the officers do not think that police use of physical force is always wrong; other data confirm this. Yet they are bothered by the dominance of unsubtle strategies of control which are used from day to day. We now consider five of these. (In the following discussion priority is accorded to crime work. My rank made it difficult for me to observe much peacekeeping work.)

Symbolic strategies

A uniformed constable standing on a street corner or driving a marked police car is representative of the pervasive character of state control (Bittner, 1970, pp. 36–51). Doubtless you will have seen a police car and checked your speedometer immediately or watched an officer looking in your direction and wondered if you were the focus of interest. The police are a highly visible symbol of the political state.

In police work any separation of symbolism from instrumentalism is tenuous and analytical. A uniformed sergeant, temporarily employed in plain clothes, parks his car outside the station, leaving his truncheon on the rear seat, to him a symbol of control. An inspector notices the truncheon and is concerned about the sergeant abusing his authority: 'I don't know what he is trying to prove, but there's a Paddy going to nick his truncheon which is on the back seat round there.' A marked police car can also be used in a symbolic manner. Using the distinctive illuminated 'Police' sign on the roof of his Panda car, an officer creates a setting in which his ability to control a motorist is first enhanced and then normalized.

> During a night-duty shift I patrolled as a passenger in a Panda, driven by a constable. We patrolled a well-lit street without the 'Police' sign illuminated. A car tried to overtake us at what the constable thought was an inappropriate moment. He switched the 'Police' sign on and said to me, 'I'll just let him know what's what.' Later he was patrolling with the sign fully illuminated. He noticed a vehicle being driven in an erratic manner and commented that the driver might have been drinking. As our car was positioned behind the suspect vehicle, the illuminated sign was switched off, making it virtually impossible for the suspect to realize the identity of the vehicle following him.

Control is here extended beyond, and then contracted to frame, the normal spatial boundaries of the car itself.

Symbols, then, extend an idea, a principle or some other notion beyond particular restrictive boundaries to a broader terrain. They penetrate physical and psychological barriers. In the following incident a uniform is used to extend police control beyond the physical frame of the officer, beyond a police vehicle, into a distant area.

> At 3.30 a.m. I was patrolling with a uniformed officer who was driving an unmarked police car. A coloured man was walking slowly along the pavement of a well-lit major route. The officer slowed his car to walking pace and on two occasions passed the man at this speed, gazing at him as he passed. The officer commented, 'These coloured people

certainly ask for trouble from us. They seem to hang about and look suspicious.'

Other data suggest that the uniform, combined with a fixed gaze, enhances symbolic control (Goffman, 1971, pp. 61–71).

> We noticed a vehicle that was double-parked. – [officer] chose to draw up behind it and continually flash his headlights. The vehicle did not move and so he rang the bell on our car. The offending vehicle moved off and we eventually went past it very slowly. As we did this the officer, wearing his cap and full uniform, glanced carefully at the driver.

In other settings officers use the uniform to imply that they are willing and able to deal with a situation when, in fact, their intentions are rather different. Someone telephones Hilton to complain that a car is obstructing the entrance to his garage. It is obvious that other than spending a long time waiting for the owner of the parked car to return, which is unacceptable, symbolizing a police presence is the only viable strategy. The constable assigned to attend the scene feels that there is little point in going to the car, but his colleague tells him, 'Well, that doesn't matter. Just go along there and show the flag. Tell them you can't do anything. Just show the flag.'

The symbolism of 'showing the flag', however, cannot always be easily separated from the aim of achieving a definite objective. When a robbery occurs in the subdivision a sergeant suggests that the officer in charge of the CID is in favour of 'getting all the villains in the station – just to let them know who's who'. Other incidents verify that arrests are sometimes made simply to symbolize police authority and power over criminals who commit serious offences. Indeed, 'professional criminals' are said to be quite in tune with such a strategy:

> – [names officer] doesn't get civil claims against him because they [professional criminals] don't know what he knows about them. If they started complaining, then – would beat them at their own game and get them for other jobs which they were committing, and serious ones at that.

Arrests like these hint at the possibility of wider-ranging police activity; they are certainly symbolic, but their symbolism finds expression in a highly instrumental context – the custody assured by arrest.

Strategies of containment

Strategies of containment are intended to limit situations which require some control but which the police cannot contain completely. A boundary of tolerance is drawn around particular behaviour, often with some symbolic flourish to signify a measure of police authority (Rock, 1973, p. 174).

A number of 'dippings' (pickpocket offences) are reported, and in response the officer in charge of the CID allows uniformed constables to work overtime, patrolling the areas in question in plain clothes. During a chat about the CID chief, a sergeant explains the strategy of containment that he employs.

> He's as good as gold. He's OK. . . . We had a lot of dippings up at – [names location], and he wanted to stop it, and after a few days it did stop. The word got round that we were up there. Mind you, old – had a couple of sus [suspected] dippings, so that soon got around.

There is implicit acknowledgement that such patrols cannot stop the pickpocketing in the longer term; containment offers only a temporary and partial means of control. Something more than a symbolic 'showing of the flag' is offered because some arrests are made, but these are attempts to define a boundary of tolerance rather than to put an end to the offences.

In situations in which alternative strategies do not calm people who are causing trouble an arrest is sometimes made in the hope that it will contain the conflict and etch the boundary of police tolerance. On one occasion officers have been called to eject troublemakers from a party. One of them recalls:

> – [names officer] went up there and was asked to evict a bloke from a party. When he got there the bloke took a swing at him and so – [officer] chucked him down the stairs and was going to nick him for drunk and disorderly outside on the street. Then a lot of them came down and had a go, and the urgent assistance call went up three times.'

Later I had an opportunity to talk to a youth arrested at this incident. I asked him what had happened.

> Youth: 'I was just standing on the pavement.'
> SH: 'What do you mean, "just standing there"?'
> Youth: 'I was just standing there. They were having a fight with one of the blokes, and I was just standing there, and a policeman came over to the crowd and said, "You're mine, you'll do," and I got nicked and was put in the van.'
>
> Knowing the arresting officer, I repeated the account to one of his colleagues. He, in turn, repeated it to a sergeant and said, 'That sounds just about right doesn't it? Typical copper. That's just how it would have happened.'

Faced with what could have been an inflammatory incident, the PC certainly milked the event of all the drama he could but chose a strategy of control which, leaving a disorderly situation in progress, aimed at containment and a demonstration of police authority.

Containment is not restricted to highly dramatic settings:

> Two traffic division officers stop a vehicle driven by a black youth outside a club frequented by blacks. They suspect the car is stolen and bring the driver and passengers to the station for questioning. One of them explains, 'I thought that for their good and for ours we had better bring them in, sarge. There were several others outside the club, and it was getting a bit difficult.'

Why do these officers act differently from those who dealt with the party? Perhaps it is because they are specialist traffic department officers who are less committed to the values and associated actions of the occupational culture than are their station patrol colleagues. They do not attribute as much value to action and hedonism. Their use of a containment strategy is designed to avoid conflict.

Crimes without readily identifiable victims are especially well suited to containment. A man is believed to be practising witchcraft and to be exhuming corpses from a local cemetery. An officer alleges that he also 'kills cats and drinks their blood'.

The press give him publicity and the Chief Superintendent gets into trouble. Our job is really to get rid of him, strip him naked and send him over the fence or send him over on to – [names bordering subdivision] ground and get rid of him that way.

Homosexuals are subject to broadly similar tactics:

While on patrol with a colleague I passed a public toilet where homosexuals were known to congregate throughout the day and night. My colleague looked at the toilet building and said, 'There's a couple having a right old wank in there. Two heads very close together.' He said no more, but when we soon passed another toilet, known to function in the same way, he mentioned a greengrocer who was known to visit the toilet frequently while on his way home from a wholesale market. 'I think I will have his van towed away sometime so that he will have to claim it. It will be a bit of a laugh anyway.'

Again, these are situations which would probably not be permanently resolved if an arrest were made; the crimes are difficult to detect but the police feel that they must do something about them and contain the situation, hoping that their action will provide sufficient warning.

Arrest and/or detention are not the only ploys used. When officers face situations in which their effort is likely to exceed the calculated benefits, they are often prompted to consider strategies of containment. This is particularly true if a considerable amount of documentation is required. Road traffic accidents are an example. As one officer puts it:

I usually try to square them up unless there is some allegation. In that one [refers to accident he has just dealt with] the damage is more than the cost of the fine, so you pays your money and you takes your choice.

Further, containment can simply mean restraint. If someone who is mentally ill acts in a strange manner, it is clear that the police will not be able to change matters; they can only contain them. The moral culpability of the person is also in doubt. On occasions when patients have to be returned to mental hospitals it is noticeable that restraint rather than force is used: ' – [names officer] has the patter. He'll go with him.' In a similar situation a supervisory officer tells his constables, 'Just restrain him, just restrain him.'

'Conning' and lying

The police always have a head start on us. We do not know how much information they have about us or how they might use what information they have. This access to private and potentially damaging information drives a wedge of uncertainty between police and public, which officers can manipulate to their advantage by 'conning' and lying (Manning, 1978). The difference between these is a fine one, save that lying involves more malice.

People are conned so that the police can settle a situation that could get out of hand. Pop music concerts which attract hundreds of young people are frequently held at a local theatre. They queue for ages waiting for a ticket, spilling on to the pavement outside the theatre. On one occasion I go to the theatre with an inspector, who asks his constables to disperse a sizeable crowd because all the available tickets have been sold. After the bulk of the crowd has dispersed he tells me:

> Oh well, they will probably only come back again, but that has done the job for the moment. . . . They are very good in there. They still have fifty tickets to sell, and if any of the lads want one, they will sell them; just ring up.

Not all police work relies on illusion. It is possible to make an arrest by lying and conning. An officer holds two warrants for a suspect. One orders a fine to be paid on the spot; the other stipulates arrest with bail and appears the more serious. The officer explains: 'He can pay the money on the first one, and he can be granted bail on the second . . . but I'll show him the second one first.' Similarly, arrests can be made by telling people merely that they are required to come to the station, without any intimation that once there they will be questioned or charged with a specific offence.

> A woman is arrested for assault and she challenges the arresting officer: 'Well have I been arrested? Am I going to be charged? You only asked me to come down here to see about it. Am I being charged, then? Am I staying in all night? I want to get back home.'

The woman was later questioned and charged with a substantive offence; the arrest strategy ensured a minimum of trouble for the officer.

Finally, a con or lie can be used to protect an informant from the possible reprisals of an offender about whom he has given incriminating evidence.

> After a youth was arrested for a burglary I asked the arresting officer for the evidence of offence and arrest in the presence of the suspect. I also asked, 'Have you got a statement?'
>
> The officer mouthed silently, 'Yes, it was made by the other bloke.' After the suspect was put in a detention room he explained his unwillingness to provide all the evidence in the presence of the suspect: 'The other kid made a statement under caution implicating him. Would you like to read it?'

Verbal control and threat

Egon Bittner (1970, p. 46) argues that the central unifying feature of policing is the capacity of an officer to use 'non-negotiably coercive force employed in accordance with the dictates of an intuitive grasp of situational exigencies'. In the most mundane of encounters this access to force operates as a threat to strengthen the control that an officer is able to exert.

Shouting a threat is sometimes an adequate means of exercising control. Some youths are messing about outside the local theatre: 'Pack it up or you'll get nicked.' After dealing with a call to 'suspects in an empty house', the information log is marked up with the result: 'Two satisfactory stops'. I ask one of the officers for a more comprehensive explanation. 'Well, I'll quote – [other officer], shall I?' "Fuck off or you'll get nicked." '

The threat is not always one of possible arrest. Within the space of thirty minutes an officer stops two drivers who, he

suspects, have been drinking. The first, a woman, is cautioned.
The second, a man who has driven at high speed, is stopped. The
officer mutters: 'I'll give him a blow, just to show him.' The
threat of possible prosecution is used, although the officer knows
that the man has not drunk enough alcohol to warrant his action.
In other situations this non-negotiable threat can involve physical force.

> After a rather long observation during the early hours of the
> morning, two constables watch a man go into a school
> playground and steal some milk. At some stage of the arrest
> he hides in the school grounds and the officer uses a threat
> to finalize the apprehension. He shouts, 'We'll put the dogs
> in after you if you don't come out.'
> 'Do you know,' he later remarks, 'he jumped straight
> back out again.'

Prosecution and physical force are just two of the resources on
which officers draw. A further expedient is to draw the suspect's
attention to the implications of a court case. An inspector and a
constable are discussing a difficult traffic case for which more
evidence is required. They particularly need the name of the
driver of a vehicle and consider using a threat: 'We'll go along
and tell him that if he doesn't give us the name, he can get two
years. Yes, that's good, we can do that.'

Of course, a threat need not relate to bona fide legal power. I
am with an inspector who wants to stop some striking employees
from blocking the road. They are cheeky, and he invites three of
them to talk by his car. When he gets to the car he opens its back
door asking, 'Do you want a seat?' They explain that the gathering is about to disperse – and it does.

Such threats permit officers some measure of control. They
are sometimes symbolic, sometimes more instrumental; sometimes they are combined with conning people. Whatever the
tactic, the threat of the non-negotiable power that is available to
police underpins this strategy.

Education and punishment

All of the strategies which have been described contain an element of education and punishment. However, there are occa-

sions when officers are more explicit about the sufficiency of these objectives.

A constable is called to deal with a woman who has been stabbed in the hand by her husband. She goes to the local magistrates' court and is advised to return to the police station for assistance with an application for a warrant of arrest. It is then discovered that the officer who dealt with the incident and recorded his action as 'Advice given' actually left the conflict because he thought that the couple should face the consequences of their dispute, not least because they seemed to take no notice of his attempts to quieten them. This strategy of education by default is more clearly illustrated by another incident:

I was patrolling with a colleague and saw four young people – two girls and two boys – arguing and scrapping on the pavement. One of the males hit a girl in the face and her nose started to bleed. My colleague drove to them quickly and asked the girl what was happening. He then turned to the boy, and as his account was being given, the girl began to shout and argue. The officer said, 'Look, I'll talk with you if you speak one at a time, but if not, I'm wasting my time.'

The boy started talking and the girl began shouting again. Officer: 'Look, you obviously aren't going to tell me. If you want to get on with it, get on with it yourselves. I'm not bothered.'

He then went to his car and as he drove away said to me, 'What's the point of me standing there and listening? I can't get anywhere when they do that, can I?'

Much later, in the early hours of the morning, another officer reported over the personal radio system that he might require some assistance to arrest a youth who, so a female told him, had threatened her with a knife. The officer who dealt with the initial incident recognized the parties concerned as those whom he had tried to control and he replied, 'No, we were there when the first blow was struck. It's just an argument between themselves. I don't know about knives, but they'd been to a party and they're just having an argument. I'd leave it if I were you.'

By absenting themselves these officers leave people to educate and/or punish each other. The police officers are involved, but their strategy is to allow disorderly people to face the consequences of the tangles into which they get themselves.

On other occasions officers are somewhat more active in fulfilling their educational task. A schoolboy had been caught writing on the wall of a cinema. The officers who caught him made him wash the slogan off with hot water and a scrubbing brush, a reprisal that was both educational and demanding, as was the following tactic when some demonstrators who sat in a road were removed;

> There was a bloody great puddle by the side of the road, and when they were nicked they were swept right through this puddle. At the nick they refused to speak English, so [the officers] just said, 'Unless you speak English you don't go home,' and they began speaking it straight away.

All of these strategies have to be related to the legal powers afforded the police; this much is basic and given (McBarnet, 1981a). Recent research by Doreen McBarnet suggests that all of the strategies that the police adopt in crimework and tasks related to it are not deviations from, but acceptable within, our very flexible framework of law. However, it is also important to take into account the rationale of the officers who appear in these cameos of police work. They are less certain that their actions are acceptable to the courts, senior officers or the local population. The apparent confidence of Hilton's officers veils hesitation about making their working rules and practices known. The PC who argues, 'It all depends on who is boss out there' indicates a touchstone of policy at Hilton – 'This is a place inhabited by people who are going to get out of hand if we don't do something.' By one strategy or another, by one tactic or another, the appearance of police control – or more precisely, as far as our officers are concerned, the reality of control – is maintained.

All strategies and tactics are supported by this fundamental view and by specific aspects of knowledge about 'prisoners' and figures. The strategies emphasize control, hedonism, action and challenge – constituents of the occupational culture. These cultural strands of policing are woven together as practical skills employed on the streets. They may provoke a critical response;

however, as far as possible, in the first instance, we have to see things from a police perspective. Nevertheless, these strategies seem to distance Hilton's officers from the constraints of legal rules and force directives, from the criticisms of the public that is policed, from the influence of the least powerful groups living and working in Hilton. Hilton's rank-and-file officers are free to police in their own style, with their own assumptions and strategies intact.

8

The Challenge of Investigation

The sensitivity of the police to their control over Hilton has been emphasized; we have reviewed their control over territory, over persons arrested and held in custody, over the process of questioning and charging. Some of the strategies and tactics used to deal with criminal and other offences on the street and something of the character of the charge-room area of the station have already been described. Now I want to return to the station and to illustrate further how suspects are handled in the charge room, and particularly how confessions of guilt are obtained. In this context of privacy, the police assumption of control and a stress on obtaining a speedy confession of guilt are paramount.

Most suspects pose no problems; they are quiet, admit their guilt and acquiesce to the evidence against them (Royal Commission, 1980; McConville and Baldwin, 1982). However, some do present difficulties, and although they are few in number, their importance is considerable. The way in which they are handled demonstrates the assumptions that are made about the role of the police in the questioning and charging process, as well as illustrating a further range of strategies of practical policemanship.

Confession

Suspects held in the station have to be respectful, quiet and generally compliant, as we have noted. There is no need to go over this ground again, except to stress that what could be interpreted as a series of highly dramatic and symbolic actions by the police, amounting to little more than 'mouth and trousers', often have an instrumental objective – the admission of guilt and a statement of confession. While orderly control within the charge room at Hilton is essential to the officers working there, the strategies they employ are designed to create uncertainty, consciousness of an imbalance of power and, possibly, a sense of fear in a suspect's mind. Officers require prisoners to admit to their offences, and they employ various strategies to that end.

The following incident illustrates that control can be exercised in a dramatic fashion but lifted once a confession has been obtained.

> After a short chase (there were suggestions that the pursuit was more imaginary than real), a youth was arrested for taking a motor car. Five officers came to the charge room with the prisoner, and they encircled him as the arresting officer said, 'In future you stop, you stop. You've learnt your lesson now, but when you're told to stop, you stop.'
>
> The youth admitted his offence and, in a serious tone, one of the other constables said, 'It's really nice to hear someone admit nowadays. I reckon he ought to be given ten pounds out of the poor box.'

A written statement in which guilt is acknowledged is certainly a priority; the CID have no doubt about how essential this is. They have to be told of every arrest made on night duty and of serious offences committed during other shifts. The purpose of calling on them is not so much to draw on their expertise in gathering further relevant evidence but rather to get a written statement of guilt. As one of them put it after 'questioning' a suspect: 'Always get a statement under caution. Always get a statement.' Even when it is not strictly necessary to get a statement under caution, CID officers choose to seek one from a prisoner; they often seem more concerned about this than about collating any broader body of evidence (Greenwood et al., 1977; McConville and Baldwin, 1982).

> The CID crew of a patrol car witnessed a burglary and also had the evidence of an independent witness who was present at the scene of the crime. Instead of assembling their

evidence of the offence as soon as they arrived at the station, they began taking statements of confession from their prisoners.

Uniformed officers are not wholly content with this approach, particularly the satisfaction of the CID with an admission of guilt to the exclusion of other evidence. The PCs believe that it tends to confuse what has actually happened in an incident. One of them remarked:

> We had some in for a snatch, and it was really unusual because we got statements out of them. Even that nearly went bent on us because the CID insisted that we charge them all with theft. But in our statements and their statements we found that only one was involved in the snatch and the other two were only there when he handed the money out. So we had to quickly charge them with dishonest handling. And they pleaded to it, but it nearly went bent because of the CID.

Of course, the decision to work like this is not based simply on failure to take note of the content of a statement. The point is that the atmosphere of investigation makes confession of guilt a priority, which relegates the careful assembly of evidence to second place. This might seem an obvious and proper procedure – but there is perhaps a difference between seeking evidence of the truth and employing a range of strategies designed to secure a verbal confession within the confines of the station.

Creating uncertainty and dependence

For one reason or another, some suspects do not readily confess their guilt. The power of the police comes into play at this point; uncertainty can be created in a suspect's mind, a sense of dependence on an investigating officer stressed. The physical setting of the charge room itself is imposing. It is a 'sanctuary' where, as Mike Chatterton (1975b, p. 296) has put it, 'The prisoner could not [fail] to [be] impressed by the formality and the power of a scene which [makes] them feel insignificant.' This relationship of power can be enhanced by emphasizing a suspect's isolation.

A husband and wife were suspected of overstaying their permission to remain in this country. They were separated by the arresting officer and placed in the detention rooms. The officer then exploited the time element, explaining to a colleague, 'She is a liar and I want the truth to sink in a bit.'

A PC informed his station officer, 'I'll tell him [a suspect] that he is going to be kept here until he tells us the truth.'
    Sergeant: 'Well, he is going to be kept here anyway.'
    PC: 'I know, but I will tell him that anyway.'

Isolation can be preceded by a host of other strategies.

A boy had been arrested for suspected theft, and he would not admit to any offence. The station officer went to the charge room as soon as he was brought to the station, and the arresting officer said, 'Sarge, this is the boy. I told him that if he tells us the truth and is a good boy, then he can go home. He's got to tell us the truth.'
    The strategy of bargaining had no effect, and questioning became more aggressive as the arresting officer was joined by a colleague. The officers moved very close to the boy as they accused him of lying and began a process of degradation.
    Officer: 'You're not a pretty boy, are you?'
    No reply.
    Officer: 'You're not a pretty boy, are you?'
    Boy: 'Yes.'
    Officer: 'I'll tell you something. You see that door over there? [Points to door of detention room.] That's where we put naughty boys like you, but we put men, naughty men, over there, in those cells there. Do you want to go in one of those cells?' He took the boy to the doorway of a cell and, out of my hearing, said something. The boy soon returned and the officer said, 'Well, he's having it now. . . . Well, that's OK, we will get a statement under caution from him.'

A similar strategy is employed when three youths are arrested and do not admit their guilt. When one of them says that he wants to admit the offence he is left in isolation, and his admission is not accepted. The principle is that the pressure on him to implicate his friend increases.

After initial questioning the station officer told the arresting officers, 'I don't think they are going to come across with very much. We'll have to give them a bit of the old "uppity".' I left the charge room and have no evidence of what followed that statement. However, later the station officer said, 'I think we will go down and tell them [they were detained in detention rooms and a cell] what we can get them for.'

The driver of the car soon told the station officer that he had given a false name and wanted to admit his fault. This was thought insufficient because the officer required a full confession. He told the youth: 'Well, you keep on thinking about what you have told me and tell me the whole truth.'

He shut the detention room door immediately. No confession was forthcoming, and the dependency and power of the police was emphasized again. 'You see, time is on our side. I'm going home to bed soon, and I can't be bothered with you being here. You can stay here until as long as we have got the truth.'

These various strategies of isolation, threat and so on combine to draw a suspect's attention to the very restrictive conditions in which he is being held. Once he becomes aware of his capture and isolated position, any information an officer has about him or his offence can be manipulated to create the impression that more is known about him than is actually the case. The balance of the situation may then be tipped to encourage a confession.

Two youths are arrested, suspected of the theft of a radio found in their possession. Once in the station they are separated in different cells and, after initial questioning fails to provide the necessary evidence, a CID officer is called. He moves very close to one of the suspects, invading his personal space, and says, 'Come on now, old son, you know about this radio. Don't think I was born yesterday 'cause I wasn't. It's better to tell me where it came from than having to tell the magistrates that you wouldn't say where it came from, now isn't it?' The suspect soon confesses and is asked: 'And you are going to make a statement, aren't you?' He does.

The other prisoner denies his involvement in any offence,

and the CID officer goes to him, creating suspicion in his mind. 'Look, son, he has told us where it has come from and that you knew it was nicked. Come on, now, you should tell us yourself.' The youth continues to deny the offence. Officer: 'Look, I don't want to get angry because he told us what it's all about. I know it's nicked. You will stay here till we find out; it's only a matter of time.' A confession is soon forthcoming.

The uniformed officer who made this arrest thinks advantage is gained by using a plain-clothes colleague:

I think that they don't know what is happening when they have a plain-clothes officer questioning them. They know who we are, but they don't know who they are talking to when they have a CID in plain clothes.

No matter how slight the information about a suspect or offence, an investigating officer is able to mould his knowledge to advantage. A hint that the case will be presented favourably to the court can help to clarify details of the current offence and others.

. . . he's all right down there [in the cells]. Nothing is happening to him. Leave him for a bit because he is just opening up to – [names officer]. We told him we could help him, and he's telling – [officer] some names of people involved in the robberies. We know some already, but new names as well.

All of these ploys heighten the challenge of investigation. Stories of elaborate incidents survive and are occasionally recounted. The following tale has an almost folklore quality. At root, the creation and sustaining of suspicion and uncertainty in the mind of the suspect forms the basis of the questioning. A PC explains;

I knew he had done a chap on our ground, so I nicked him for it and brought him in. I couldn't prove it, so I said to him that there was some luminous paint on the roof within the last six months it would show up under the special lamp. So

I went and got some crayon that – [names crime prevention officer] uses and rubbed it in my hands. Then I rubbed the charge room bench with it and said, 'Sit down there,' right where the crayon was. Then I touched him on the shoulder and rubbed my hand on his sleeve. Of course, when we came to put the jacket under the lamp it was brilliant. He couldn't believe it. He had to put his hands up. Yes, I did that one by subterfuge. Then I started on the cars; he wouldn't have it, and I was with him from 7 p.m. to 4 a.m. So I just let him go and told him to come and see me the next morning. In he comes and I just go through our crime book and clear up a load. Seven pages of statement under caution by the time I've finished. Cars from all over.

All the usual embellishment has gone into this account, but the point about the challenge of creating suspicion and uncertainty remains. As with other aspects of policing at Hilton, we find the assumptions of working policemen dominate the process of investigation. These assumptions contrast with the idea of questioning as a slow accumulation of evidence from a number of sources, including meticulous questioning of a suspect. The speedy extraction of a confession of guilt takes precedence over Judges' Rules and other protective instruments of law. The strategies used cohere around the notion of control, strengthening and harmonizing the framework of discretionary freedom that the lower ranks identify as properly their own.

'Verballing' and the adjustment of evidence

A 'verbal' is an oral statement of admission or incrimination which is invented by the arresting or interviewing officer and attributed to a suspect (Powis, 1977). A verbal is a lie, and its use in evidence is illegal, which, to say the least, makes the writing of this section rather tricky and open to all manner of misreading. At Hilton it is evidently the case that officers do not routinely verbal suspects; none of the following discussion suggests as much. However, comments about verballing are made at Hilton; cases in which verballing is said to have taken place create interest among officers. We need to know how a strategy like this is able to survive in the context of routine policing.

A starting-point is provided by an officer who does not work at Hilton and who says that he does not construct evidence or lie in the witness box. Nevertheless, when he describes a special constable from his station he implies that verballing can be considered an aspect of effective policemanship: 'Now, he is a good one, he's like a real copper. Gets in the box and swears white is black and all that routine.' 'A real copper' – his description is probably exaggerated, but it does imply that officers do not regard verballing as extraordinary. Indeed, it is possible for a CID officer who is assisting with a case of attempted burglary to suggest to an arresting officer, 'I don't want to push you or anything, but I do think that we should have some verbal evidence to tie him up with the implement.' The officers' refusal to agree to this ploy is not regarded as weakness, bad practice or unacceptable. The 'advice' merely indicates that it is quite possible for the question of verballing to be raised during routine work.

The following incident concerns a constable who has been returned to patrol duty from a special crime squad. I wondered if his return was a consequence of his reluctance to verbal, to 'work the oracle' as it is sometimes called, and I asked a colleague:

'Was it that he was not willing to put the verbal in? To work the oracle?'

He replied, 'It might have been that, it is necessary at times but I don't think that he had much idea about what was what – that's all.'

During this conversation I asked about two officers replacing the constable.

SH: 'Who selected – for the squad?'

Officer: 'The officer in charge did. He was allowed to have who he wanted and he chose – and –.

SH: 'They are likely to end up in the dock for perjury, aren't they?'

Officer: 'Yes, I suppose they are, but – had the free hand to choose who he wanted.'

In this context of a more specialist crime squad, staffed by uniformed personnel, the possibility of verballing remains. Indeed, other data suggest that the officer described as 'not knowing what's what' has a rather different and less adaptive view of policing than have his colleagues on the squad, not least the one who replaces him.

Again, the point is the tacit acceptance by many officers of verballing as necessary on some occasions. A rather different tactic is stressed when an officer is told not to verbal but to make an arrest.

> They nicked a bloke for – [names offence]. I don't reckon that they [others present were also arrested] should ever have been nicked at all. [After arrival at the station] Sergeant – told me that I had to have one of them. I said that I didn't nick anybody, but he told me that I had to have one of them. I told him again, but he told me that I was a probationer and that I needed them for figures and I couldn't afford not to take a body. I had to take him and that right upset me, that put me back. It's just like – [names another officer]. He was there and he keeps reminding me about it and taking the mickey. He says that you can't argue when you are a probationer. You have to do as you are told and take the bodies that you are told to take. It just upsets me.

Although this young constable is unhappy about this arrest, a refusal to verbal does not usually result in harsh criticism from colleagues; disagreement is tolerated. The basic morality, if not the practice, of verballing remains intact; however, the criticism does not remove verballing from the armoury of investigation.

> Two officers from Hilton had disturbed some youths who were on the verge of stealing a motor car. They were arrested and taken to the local station, some distance from Hilton. During the arrest, reported over the radio system, several officers from Hilton joined their colleagues and discussed the issue when they returned.
>
> PC: 'Refused charge by the station officer over there. – [names officer] wasn't willing to say that little extra. They were out to nick a vehicle all right, they admit it but they were just acting as look-outs.'
>
> Colleagues: 'So he wouldn't say the old sparkler?'
>
> PC: 'No, he doesn't believe in that sort of thing, so it's fair

enough. Only trouble was that I was about to take a statement under caution.' This officer then turned to another
colleague and offered a further explanation: 'And it is a
foreign court anyway, so there we are. You see, he doesn't
believe in that sort of thing so, after all, that's fair, isn't it?'

Colleague: 'Yes.'

The officer who made the arrests soon returned to
Hilton, where his colleagues were still assembled. He was
asked, 'What went wrong?'

'We came along a couple of minutes too early.'

'I suppose it is a foreign court.'

'No, – [names officer involved] was of the same opinion
as me. No, it's not just that.'

A similar situation is created when an officer, who is much less
popular than his colleague mentioned in this incident, arrests
some men for 'gross':

Three men were arrested in the early hours of the morning
for 'gross indecency'. There was little evidence against
them and one complained bitterly that he had been arrested
unlawfully. When I told another sergeant that there was
insufficient evidence to charge them, he said, 'He [the
arresting constable] will just have to change the evidence,
won't he?'.

I said, 'No, he won't,' but when he saw the arresting
officer my colleague repeated his remark.

The arresting officer declined his advice, 'I only see what
I see.'

In fact, the inspector who dealt with the matter refused
the charge, but this did not prevent some of the constables
who were present in the station from expressing their
views: 'He . . . is a fool for not changing his story.'

Another pointed to the fact that his colleague was not
acting in a commonsense manner: 'I am not going to tell
you what to do. I'm not going to tell you how to suck eggs,
am I?'

The issue of verballing is therefore a live one and can press in
upon an officer at any time.

Legitimation

Why are some policemen apparently willing to consider and be uncritical about verballing? Does the sergeant who has served at Hilton for many years not present good reason to desist?

> Not me. If I get anything it is straight. . . . If you put words in people's mouths, you are supporting bad law, and there is no need for it half the time. Once these youngsters get into the habit of getting into that, you don't know where it is going to stop.

So how is this strategy legitimated? What reasons are given for its use, prompting its tacit acceptance among some of Hilton's ranks?

When a verbal or a similar strategy is used, a suspect's guilt is assumed and so, therefore, is a proper conviction by a court. By strategies like verballing the criminal justice system is conflated into a single act, in the course of which arrest, guilt and conviction are all assumed. The law is deemed inadequate to secure acknowledgement of guilt and conviction, which means that the legal constraints of the rule of law have to be ignored and neutralized (Matza, 1964). Officers suppose that they have access to privileged knowledge because they 'know' that the suspect is guilty and therefore accept some responsibility for seeing that justice is done, even if that means helping the evidence along a little.

> I verbal people, and I think that it is justified. If we are given laws which can't be put into practice, then we have to try and make them work, and this means verballing. Look at 'offensive weapons'. You are almost obliged to give the prisoner a verbal to get a conviction on that charge. . . . I take the oath, but to me it might as well be swearing on any old bit of paper. It doesn't mean anything to me. I don't have to say that I believe in it. . . . I think I am fair to people.

A similar view is expressed by another PC:

> when you have a legal system that allows people to get off

and makes you break the law to get convictions, then you have to be slightly bent.

Both these officers legitimize verballing by attributing moral responsibility for their actions to a general and impersonal artifact, the legal system; personal failing is minimized because verballing is considered virtually inevitable.

A related point is that officers do not think that verballing involves the wholesale fabrication of evidence. Adjustments, refinements and corrections are made to render the suspect's guilt more obvious – they 'gild the lily' rather than create guilt and a conviction from nothing. Remember, from this police perspective, suspects are guilty and are often not offended by verballing. An officer explains:

> Well, you manufacture the evidence. Couldn't get in there. Only – [names race] are allowed in there, so I manufactured the evidence. They pleaded guilty. They knew they were guilty. So that was that.

'Professional criminals' and/or 'villains' (that is, persistent, cunning and dangerous offenders) are singled out as particularly suited to verballing. They know the working rules of this game of investigation; if the police don't keep to them, their opponents will laugh. Comment is made about an officer who has recently been transferred from a squad which deals with these types of offender:

> 'It's because people like – [names officer] are willing to put their necks out in court to get these blokes down, or else you'd never do it. They'd be laughing at you if you didn't do it. You'd never get anybody convicted.'
>
> I contested again, arguing that the law, not evidence, should be changed.
>
> This argument was countered: 'Law can't change that. It's part of being a policeman. If you know they're guilty, there's nothing wrong, and if you're not willing to do it, you shouldn't be in the job.'

'Villains' are mentioned again by an officer who comments about an arrest made by a colleague:

I was told, 'Now this is a case where a good verbal is needed
. . . and not out of place. He's a right villain, this one.'

What is so striking here is the officers' readiness to accept the
risk entailed when a verbal is used. The legitimations
themselves promote some measure of confidence, which is
further strengthened by a general but usually muted appreciation:

> I don't care what you think. . . . I know we will disagree here
> but, you know, I somehow admire blokes who do it. You get
> real big villains, and you know that they have done some-
> thing, and the only way to get him down is to gild the lily
> against him, you know? I don't think blokes do it easily;
> they don't, they worry about it. They worry about it as the
> case is coming to court and they are glad it is over and it is
> not easy for anybody. They don't enjoy it, but they think it is
> necessary to do it if they are going to convict these people,
> and that is what they are going to do.

However, supportive as these comments might seem, verballing
still provokes a sense of unease. On their own, the legitimations of
verballing are not sufficient, and other structural features of the
occupational culture assume importance.

Trust, teamwork and secrecy

An officer who is going to use a verbal has to trust any colleagues
who may know what he is doing. Corroboration and/or secrecy
have to be assured; trust cannot be secured unless a colleague
shows an initial willingness to verbal:

> We found an axe under the front seat, but I couldn't get him
> to say the right words, and there was nothing I could do
> about it. – [names officer] is a bit naive.

Caution is also expressed about civilian witnesses who may not
be telling the truth. Officers have no idea if they can trust them
and take care not to be implicated in shaky jobs of this sort. One
of the store detectives who works at Hilton is suspected of being
less than truthful:

'I agree, she doesn't see all that she says she sees. She stands by the door and looks at people going out, and anyone who looks the type, she just stops them. Well, 99 per cent of the time she's right, but of course she's not right all the time.'

... 'Yes, where there's evidence I don't think you have got much choice but to take the charge, but I refused one of them. As I say, I always take a personal interest if the person denies it.'

Women can disarm the police, as we have noted, and this fact may be reflected in the comments about the store detective. However, the trust which is essential among police colleagues is also absent, which makes the officers wary of her evidence. For similar reasons, questioning that takes place through an interpreter also prevents verballing. An officer who has already been quoted as saying that he is not averse to verballing makes the point:

I know you might not agree with this, but when you know that someone has done something wrong and you are questioning them, you can put the right answers down, put the right verbals in. But when there is an interpreter you can't do that.

Trust among colleagues is vital; it is fostered by the teamwork character of policing. The idea of being a member of a police team helps to bind the work group together, and this has particular implications for the supervision of the charge room.

When an arrest is made the suspect is taken to the charge room, where the station officer, usually a sergeant or an inspector, hears all the available evidence. Station officers have been constables; they know about the use of verbals and must suspect that some of the evidence presented to them is likely to be embellished or false. In fact, there is little they can do if they suspect that evidence provided by a colleague is untrue. An investigation would usually amount to conflict between an officer's word and that of a suspect; the court is the place for such disputes. Nevertheless, the interdependence among the police team, to which the station officer belongs, makes it slightly more difficult for him to question the validity of evidence. He is expected to support his colleagues – his team mates – and is dependent upon them for co-operation in his own work. A station officer makes this point more clearly:

> If I do a job, it is straight. There is not any other routine. When I do it, it's straight down the line, and that's the end to it. Mind you, if a PC wants to come to me with full evidence, then that's it. Nothing I can do about that. As far as I am concerned, my jobs are straight.

Other station officers who may be more sympathetic to the use of a verbal can create a certain setting in the charge room which indicates that their investigation of evidence will require further detail. The use of evasive language suggests that a verbal must not be admitted but might be appropriate, as is evident from the following incident. The station officer had refused a charge of 'offensive weapon' for lack of evidence. However, as he made his written entry in the appropriate book:

> one of the PCs said to me, 'There's evidence of drunk and dis, sarge.'
> I said, 'As far as I am concerned I need evidence, and you must give me the evidence. You've got to prove it in court and give me the evidence.' So they gave me all the evidence, just like in training school, and they did their reports perfect. So it's down to them as far as I am concerned. I don't know what happened in court.

Another station officer suggests a similar ploy when he describes how he has dealt with a charge.

> I never tell the PC to verbal them. I just say, 'Did he say anything?'. If they don't, OK.

Although the structure of the police team tends to bind officers together, it cannot offer complete protection from the consequences of verballing. At Hilton it is unusual for a station officer to require evidence of drunk and disorderly. The reversion to formal procedures when it seems that some fabrication of evidence might occur may be protection for the station officer, who indicates to his PCs that they must take full responsibility for their actions; if they are disciplined, he cannot be implicated (Bittner, 1965).

Dependency among the shift of officers extends beyond ties of loyalty between the constables and sergeants to include inspectors in charge of a relief. They are also part of the web of trust and teamwork, though one step removed from the field of play:

> After a person had been charged with being drunk and disorderly I commented in the presence of the inspector in charge of the relief that I did not think the man was drunk. The inspector said, 'You shouldn't be saying that out loud, sarge. You shouldn't be saying that out loud.'

A rather different piece of evidence makes this same point.

> An inspector was in the office with constables who had arrested a youth for taking a motor vehicle. He had been present at the arrest. One of the arresting officers said, 'See what I've put down for when he was nicked?'
>
> PC2: 'Oh, I heard him say that, oh yes.'
>
> Inspector: 'In between other things.' He laughed loudly.
>
> PC2: 'Did you caution him?' Laughter again.
>
> PC3: 'I'll say I did, I saw the boot going·in. We were only one car's length behind him, and before I could get out I saw six policemen had jumped on him.'

Along with trust and the interdependency of teamwork, secrecy assists the adaptation of evidence. Secrecy among rank-and-file officers has already been stressed, and its impact on the manner in which prisoners are handled is considerable. If there is a risk that under the stress of the court hearing an officer may be unable to maintain his composure, he should not consider using a verbal. Secrecy is essential. A sergeant with many years of service behind him makes this clear during a conversation between myself and another sergeant:

> 1st sergeant: He [SH] says you shouldn't tell lies in the witness box, the fucking idiot.'
>
> 2nd sergeant: 'Well, it's no good trying to do it because every time I try I go bright red. I'd hate to have a job at Sessions where I'd have to tell lies. I don't think I could do

it. Well, I can't do it because I know as soon as it starts coming I go brilliant red. I can tell little ones, little white lies, but I can't tell proper lies. Much as at times I would have liked to have told a lie, I just can't do it.'

Rehearsals of a court hearing can shore up any weak points in the evidence which may appear in court.

Two officers were sitting in the station office writing their notes for a court case due to be heard the following morning. Their evidence concerned an arrest they had made some time before the notes were compiled. Many of their colleagues were also in the station office. One commented to the other: 'I've got more in my book than you.' He laughed.

The other officer held his notebook and showed a blank page. He said, 'Well, have you got the verbals?'

Another officer said, 'I don't think I should be hearing this.'

There was general laughter and another colleague asked one of the officers who was making his notes, 'Officer, when did you make these notes?'

He answered, 'At the time, sir.'

Further laughter followed, and the officers completed their notes.

During the rehearsal trust is tested, secrecy reinforced and teamwork strengthened; if there are flaws in the evidence or the performance, repair work is carried out to ensure an appearance of legality. Fun is certainly involved, but the banter reflects the challenge presented by policing a disorderly world.

The description and analysis in this chapter does not suggest that Hilton's officers lie through their back teeth whenever they have insufficient evidence against a suspect. The number of officers who might verbal a suspect is impossible to assess; it is difficult to separate attitudes expressed in conversation from action, rumour from fact. Nevertheless, verballing remains acceptable for some, and despite a firm and general unwillingness to 'fit people up' with evidence, the structure of the work group as a team and the values of trust and secrecy combine to provide a setting within which it is possible for an officer to verbal. Verballing remains one of the strategies of the investigator. The law prohibits it; the costs of being found out are very considerable; many officers – indeed, most – do not entertain its use: yet the legitimations which rationalize its employment are equally part of the verbal currency of policing at Hilton.

Assumption of a suspect's guilt and the adjustment rather than the total fabrication of evidence tend to divert culpability from the individual officer to the inadequacy of the criminal justice system. These legitimations are strengthened by the implicit trust and secrecy among constables, sergeants and inspectors and their interdependent teamwork. The law and very strong constraints of morality are moulded in the course of routine policing to make it possible for those officers (probably very few) who verbal to do so.

9

Force as a Means of Control

For most readers of this book violence concerns other people in other places, but if we want to study policing at close quarters, we have to be willing to be close to scuffles and to fights. Suspects may find themselves on the receiving end of a police fist; policemen may face the same treatment from a suspect. Policing can be a pretty violent business, and police stations like Hilton can be violent places.

Our distaste of anything more than a verbal punch-up can easily simplify the way we think about the police use of force – 'force' because this is a less emotive term than 'violence' and more comprehensive than Al Reiss's 'police brutality' (1965). The ways in which Hilton's officers employ their legal right to 'use as much force as is necessary' to secure the arrest and detention of a suspect are complex and various. Rules concerning the use of force have specific connotations, and these have to be described and analysed within the context of the occupational culture. This social context of analysis is suggested not just by the work of sociologists but also by the research of psychologists, which suggests that there may be a few officers who are prone to resort to excessive force; the reasons for this are very uncertain (Bayley and Mendelsohn, 1968; Lefkowitz, 1975; Teahan, 1975; Toch, 1972; Toch and Schulte, 1961). However, the behaviour of these and other officers has to be understood against a background of acquiescence, if not overt support, of colleagues.

Retaining control and authority

In their separate studies of American policing Al Reiss (1965) and William Westley (1970) argue that officers use force when their authority is challenged. Reiss writes: 'Open defiance of police authority . . . is what the policeman defines as his authority, not necessarily "official authority".' In this case what seems to hold in the American setting is relevant to Britain and, more particularly, to Hilton. When the personal authority of an officer is called into question, he may use force to make a situation acceptable to him. One of Hilton's officers begins to explain: 'We got to the station and he called me "son". So I had to hit him. I had to teach him the error of his ways.' A sergeant refers to an officer from another station who, it seems, struck a prisoner recently transferred to Hilton: 'He was given a lesson in how to be polite, which was nice of – [names officer] considering that he was giving me the prisoner.' These prisoners are given a 'lesson' because they have been disrespectful; they have challenged police authority. Such challenges can take a number of different forms.

Running away from an officer is certainly an indication that you have something to hide. However, it can also be understood as an indication of disrespect:

> 'There were two spades fighting – one was kicking hell out of the other. They ran off and one was caught.'
>   Colleague: 'Suppose he got a bit of summary justice then, did he?'
>   Officer kicks his foot in the air: 'I don't know about that, but I know the one who was caught was singing like mad.'

> A prisoner who had a cut to the mouth explained his injury: 'Yes, you know why I got this. I ran away. I'll say no more, and that's where the matter ends.'

He was right – he should not have run away. Neither, if he had been in a car, should he have driven away from pursuing officers. After a short chase, already described as more of a contrivance by officers than the intention of the youth arrested:

> The officer brought the offender to the charge room and

said to him, 'In future, you stop, you stop. You've learnt your lesson now, but when you're told to stop, you just stop.' The youth had a swollen lip and nose.

Once caught, these suspects apparently resisted arrest. They may have appeared ready to fight, prompting the use of force to nip things in the bud. An explanation based solely on this sort of reasoning has to be placed alongside the more specific accounts of officers and their own interpretation of disrespect, which we find once again when a prisoner is rude to a station officer. A sergeant who has dealt with a youth in the past explains:

> He's not a kid, he's a little bastard. I'd like to thump his head in. He's a liar, he's rude, he's a villain, he goes out stealing, he goes out and does burglary, takes cars. Last time he was in here we had a hell of a time with him. He complained about me. Mind you, he got a lot of aggro back.

A solicitor has come to the station with this boy, which prevents any use of force in the privacy of the charge room. No solicitor is present, however, when a female prisoner is difficult:

> A woman who was drunk and drugged struggled as some officers tried to remove potentially injurious rings from her fingers. As she resisted, a male prisoner who was sitting nearby commented that such firm handling was not necessary. The station officer referred to the jewellery and said, 'If it wasn't a girl we would just thump her.'

In other chapters it has been indicated that force is not the only strategy which can be used to retain authority; many factors may weight the balance in its favour and were no doubt present in the examples given. However, when personal authority is challenged the framework of assumptions within which Hilton's officers work brings the possibility of physical force to the fore. Authority has to be restored and maintained.

Assaults on the police

Hitting a person who has assaulted a colleague carries overtones of self-protection and punishment. These more instrumental features of the action fuse with the symbolism of restoring the virtual sanctity of the police, which is profaned by an assault. Total police control and authority are symbolized when an officer puts his view as strongly as this: 'If anyone touches a policeman, he deserves to be hung.'

A comment by a station officer blends the symbolic and the instrumental more clearly. I ask him about the physical state of a prisoner who has struck an officer with a chair: 'Not bad really. There was a token, but he wasn't beaten up, not by any means.' A token like this extends from the individual to the wider societal context of police authority and control, which has apparently been challenged. Symbolic force also reinforces the working solidarity of officers. It weakens the threat to their occupational identity, which they think is disturbed; the grievance is redressed by the use of force when a colleague is assaulted.

This reinstatement of police authority by means of force is critical. When a suspect responsible for assaulting two officers is hit on the head with a truncheon and completely immobilized, the PCs still dominate him with their presence. The suspect is in the station, lying on the floor of the charge room, surrounded by PCs who, despite his complete inability to offer any further challenge to them, continue to ensure that he cannot move – they are wholly in charge. We find this again more clearly in the handling of a suspect who has assaulted a colleague:

> One of the PCs who was present at the incident recalled, 'She [a WPC] was saying: "Don't hit him." We said [to her], "Get in there and keep quiet." ' The officer was taken to a police vehicle and her colleagues who had made the arrest returned to the prisoner 'and . . . continued'.
>
> I asked for an explanation of this behaviour.
>
> 'Well, it's very closely knit, the police. If your brother or sister gets hurt, you do something about it. It's like your brothers and sisters.'

Trust and interdependency – the web of relationships found in the occupational culture – are reaffirmed by this instrumental but also highly symbolic use of force.

It would be stupid to suggest that there are not times when it is necessary for Hilton PCs and sergeants to hit prisoners who are assaulting them. Nevertheless, the assault of a colleague stimulates more than the instinct for self-protection because it sharpens the whole focus of policemanship and stresses its sanctity to the lower ranks. The exchange of force, the redress of control even when a suspect is unable to offer any further resistance and the affirmation of police identity are crucial as instrumental and symbolic emphases are welded together at the end of a police fist.

Questioning and confession

The importance to officers of obtaining a confession from a prisoner held in custody has already been stressed. One further strategy designed to induce confession is the threat and use of force. Like the similarly illegal strategy of verballing, the use of force during questioning is infrequent and is not expected from every officer.

> During a social studies lecture at training school, a group of sergeants were discussing Milgram's experiment on conformity, and the instructor asked the class if they conformed in response to the use of violence by colleagues. He asked: 'When somebody's getting a kicking in the charge room, what do we do? Do we conform or not?'
> One officer replied jokingly, 'It depends if we get a confession or not, doesn't it?'
> His colleagues laughed but the instructor asked again, 'Are you saying that somebody can be thumped to get a confession?'
> Officer: 'No, I'm against all that sort of thing.'
> Later when the instructor used the phrase 'when policemen thump people' he was interrupted by an officer: 'What do you mean, sir? All policemen? I think you've given yourself away there. It's not all policemen.'
> The reproof was accepted; only 'some policemen' use force when questioning suspects.

There is a tendency at Hilton to employ particular officers when difficult prisoners are questioned and it seems likely that force will have to be used. Like those who verbal, these officers are willing to accept the risks involved. The suggestion is made that if a particular CID officer is called (or, in the past, if any member of the CID assisted in questioning), force might be used.

> A doctor had complained about the number of injured prisoners from Hilton being treated at his hospital. A sergeant disagreed: 'That is a load of rubbish. Considering the number of people we get through here, I've seen very, very little of it.'
> Colleague: ' – , that CID bloke, always hits them, gives them a clip around the ear.'
> 'Yes, – [another CID officer] thumps them, but that is about all.'
> 'It always used to be that if you sent for the CID, the prisoner would get thumped around the cell, but it is not like that now.'

The sergeant's judgement is partly accurate. Before this conversation took place, one of the uniformed sergeants spoke to me about a CID officer who had helped to question a suspect.

> Yes, he hit one of my prisoners not long ago; it's always best if you only hit your own prisoner. Mind you, I had a bloke in here at that time, and I didn't lay a finger on him because I had had a few investigations against me and I didn't want any more trouble. You see, – [names officer] came along and just gave him a clip around the ear, not much, and the bloke admitted about eight offences in no time at all.

Force used in a setting like this is viewed differently from that employed after an officer has been assaulted. In the context of questioning a more measured judgement is made, which combines with, almost forms, an extension of verbal communication between the investigating officer and the prisoner. I cannot map out a detailed model sequence for those cases involving the use of force, but it seems that verbal questioning takes place first and then, depending on its results, a measure of force may be considered, threatened or used.

> Look, many times I have known prisoners who have coughed to seven or eight jobs when they have been given a

quick thump. They have been questioned for a long time and you get nowhere. Then you give them a quick slap and suddenly they sing to a whole load of other jobs. Some people respond to questioning and others to violence. A lot of them only understand and expect violence, then they sing.

You might get four yobs knocked off and they won't say anything but you know they have done something. You have to pick out the one who has a low threshold to violence, and often as soon as you intimate to him that you may use violence against him he sings. Then you go to the others and they start and you end up with the truth.

This officer then went on to describe another case:

I talked and talked to this kid, and then I took him to the detention room and gave him one sharp slap around the left ear and straight away he told me where the property was. I was able to recover the property and give some poor kid his property back, and the suspect was charged with theft. . . . Mind you, I don't agree with the indiscriminate violence towards prisoners. There is a difference between giving someone a good slap and hitting just for the sake of it. Neither am I in favour of getting evidence by putting someone in fear by the use of force.

Like language, with its stylistic and syntactic prescriptions, the use of physical force during the questioning of a prisoner seems to be governed by rules. Although an arresting officer had faced danger when he arrested a person for possession of a shotgun, a colleague indicated that he had broken the rules by using too much force to extract a confession. When the arresting officer wanted to know to whom the shotgun belonged he 'smashed [the suspect] in the face', an action to which his colleague responded with humour and criticism: 'Skilled investigation, was it?' A more regularized approach was suggested by a constable who, when discussing another case, argued:

if it was a stroppy Paddy or a right tow-rag, he would get a right-hander. But a kid, not that, just a slap round the face and 'Shut up.'

Another officer implied that he accepted a similar code when a woman falsely accused him of assaulting her son as he was being arrested. He told her:

> I can tell you that if he was a grown man and he put up that sort of struggle he'd have a black eye. But he's not. He's only a boy. What do you take me for? I wouldn't hit a boy like that.

An appropriate scale of force is suggested by this code – thumping a prisoner around will not do.

Limits to tolerance should not be exceeded during questioning. Undue force may provoke a complaint against an officer; a suspect may simply clam up. There are horses for courses when it comes to investigation, and you have to know what types of force are suited to particular suspects and offences. But no matter how complicated and sensitive the code may be, officers who are willing to hit a suspect risk disciplinary charges; supervisory staff are not meant to turn a blind eye. Many, perhaps most, do not. However, there are certain ploys which reduce the chances that an officer will be seen hitting a suspect and that a supervisory officer will be involved. It is possible to move a suspect who may have to be hit into the private space of a cell. The creation of private space in a car and within the comparatively open confines of the charge room itself has already been documented. A supervisory officer may be present but cannot actually witness events and intervene in these settings. Secrecy and security are also strengthened when no more than a few staff are involved, so that they can all cover themselves should a complaint arise and an investigation be set in motion later. Other data suggest that station officers may wait for PCs to finish their own investigation before they themselves go to the charge room. After a prisoner had viciously assaulted a PC he was brought to the station, injured but apparently still protesting. I asked the telephonist who had been on duty how the station officer dealt with the situation;

> [He] was playing cards, and when all the commotion was going on in the charge room he just continued playing cards and said, 'We'll wait until it's all quietened down,' and then he went down there and dealt with it.

The web of trust between constables includes sergeants and inspectors, as we have noted. After questioning a suspect an officer says:

'Well, at least I know that my thumb is all right now.'
Colleague: 'Didn't you feel any effects? I just had a bit of aching in my fingers.'
'No, didn't feel anything at all.' This officer then looked at the Inspector. 'Oh, hello, Inspector, ssh. . . .'
Both laughed and the inspector said, 'What?'
PC: 'He didn't have anything to do with it. We were right away on our own.'
Inspector: 'Well, did you want me there? You didn't, did you? Did you want me there?'
PC: 'No, we were quite all right, thank you. We were quite all right.'
Telephonist: 'He'd have kept away if he'd got any sense.'

It is considered safer to hit a suspect on a part of the body where bruising will not show – in the stomach, for instance – or to administer a quick slap on the face. One criticism levelled at officers who had used a truncheon on a prisoner's head was: 'Well, we have been involved in it for years, but people, of course, are hit where it doesn't show, not like it did on that kid.' Another prisoner who had been arrested on many occasions told me that he had exploited his injury by attempting to make an officer's tactical use of force more apparent:

One time I was up at – [another station] and the CID came in and hit me in the stomach where it couldn't be seen. So I just knocked my head up against a wall and cut myself all round the eye there. You can see the scar. You see, I've been nicked so many times, I know all the different ways they get at you.

If visible injury is sustained by an officer during an arrest or some other incident he can report sick, which draws attention to his own injuries and puts a prisoner's injuries into perspective. After a prisoner had been injured the arresting officer was subject to an investigation. On hearing that the PC had gone sick, an officer remarked: 'Blimey, I hope he has. That strengthens our case, doesn't it?' Of course, this remark did not imply that the constable would not be thoroughly investigated, but it demonstrates that force can be regularized in some settings.

All of these incidents occurred over a period of two years. It has to be repeated that not all officers are willing to hit prisoners except in self-defence. Yet some officers do use force, however infrequently, when questioning prisoners, and much as supervisory officers may dislike this strategy, the structure of the rank-and-file group facilitates its use and offers some measure of protection. In the face of laws which prohibit the use of force by the police, working rules sustain a notion of policemanship and its practice which makes force nonetheless a practical expedient.

Retribution

The phrase 'summary justice' is, for a change, police and not sociological jargon. It is retributive, first, because of the inadequate sentencing policy of the courts; secondly, because of an intense police identification with victims of crime. Sentencing is thought to be particularly inadequate in the juvenile court and to be frustrated by the system of cautioning used in Hilton division. A constable who is extremely reluctant to use force is discussing this point with a colleague:

> Well, what do you expect when the courts don't give proper punishment? I can tell you, a policeman comes to this station; the first one he arrests is a juvenile, or he soon arrests a juvenile because that is what happens around here. They either get a caution or they go to court and get fined a couple of bob. He soon thinks it's not worth it, and the next time he gives the kid a bit of rough justice, a bit of summary justice. I can tell you, I hear more young men around this station talking about summary justice than I've ever done.

So far as officers are concerned, punishment is meted out only to guilty people, a view that accords with Al Reiss's (1965) argument that the police and the courts contract a symbiotic relationship when force is used to punish.

I also think it is permissible to thump a prisoner and get justice. You see, we know the officer who brings the person to the station. We know some of the facts and, let's face it, we know that most people who are brought to the station are guilty anyway. So what's wrong with giving them a verbal or adding some evidence?

The courts are often thought inadequate: 'There's no punishment in it. . . . They went out of court laughing. What can you do with that?' 'Give 'em a thick ear.' Officers who make remarks like these also have to do the 'dirty work' of supporting the victims of crime. They see the hurt and distress that are the consequences of an offence. Squatters who have inhabited and badly damaged some new flats ready for occupation by pensioners, child assaulters, 'right villains' and, perhaps unusually, those who damage motor cars without apparent reason are 'possibles' for the use of force. 'Just deserts' are adjudicated and administered by Hilton's officers.

Danger and hedonism

Although the officers perceive Hilton as a disorderly rather than a dangerous place, they do occasionally find themselves faced with danger and are injured. Some injury is expected and has to be tolerated. When a probationer constable suggests that his grazed knee constitutes grounds for a charge of assault against the police, he is jokingly corrected by a more experienced colleague: 'What, you trying to swift bodies away now? Already . . .? Another put the matter this way: 'Yes, but it is a bit of fun, isn't it? A struggle. I mean, you don't expect them to come quietly, do you? It's all a bit of fun.'

In the essentially quiet and unexciting job of policing, fun has to be snatched whenever the opportunity arises, and many potentially dangerous situations in which officers can be involved in a fight have their hedonistic aspect. The very masculine character of police work, emphasizing aggression and bravado, combines with the generally hedonistic perspective of the lower ranks to magnify the importance (almost the pleasure) of fights. When a call asking for police attendance at a club catering for young blacks is received and it is thought that a fight is taking place, officers race down the stairs from the canteen shouting as if they are playing cowboys. When they describe car chases which end in the use of force against a prisoner excitement, action and fun are fundamental to the telling. Of one lengthy chase across the city, during which the commentary from the lead car was interrupted by suggestions from other officers that force should be used, this account was given:

> I listened to the radio commentary, and when the offending vehicle stopped the driver of one of the cars at the scene said, 'He's been arrested, as have the other occupants of the car. There is a bit of summary justice being handed out now.'
>
> Others joined in to encourage this use of force and headquarters had to warn officers that their remarks were being recorded and might be heard at a later date.
>
> One of Hilton's officers arrested an occupant of the offending car, and I asked him how the arrest was made.
>
> 'Well, I had to climb on the bonnet of the car, sarge, to nick him.'
>
> 'How the hell did you climb on the bonnet? Why did you have to do that?'
>
> He expalined: 'The only way we could get him out was through the windscreen. Yes, we couldn't get him out through the doors because the police cars had hemmed them all in and – [names officer] had rammed him. We just pulled him out by the front windscreen. It had been broken by the truncheons that had been thrown at it. Well, one PC was trying to pull him out of the side window, and the other two came out the back windscreen.'

In fact, the official written record of the injury – grazing to the officer's knuckles and a sprained elbow – are explained as the result of arresting a violent prisoner. Like many other chases in the course of which officers are willing to court unnecessary danger by joining the string of pursuing vehicles, force is used and action generated. The force is part of the fun. It amuses the PCs, as one of them tells his colleagues:

> Oh yes, I was the one who held the poor man's arm up his back and stamped on his cigar because you are not allowed to smoke in the food department.

When a man was being held by a number of officers who had used force to arrest him one of them commented:

> 'He was struggling, so I just clipped him straight round the ear, punched him straight round the ear. Then he says, "Pack up, you are just enjoying this, just enjoying this, hitting me." '
>
> PC: 'Yer, right on, right on.'
> Colleague: 'Yer, right.'
> PC: 'So I hit him again'.
> Colleague: 'Yes, come on, you were enjoying it and I was. It was great.'
> PC: 'Right on.'

And if duty at the local football match offers the action of a fight, you can, as one of the PCs put it, have 'a right punch-up' – 'It should be pretty good.'

In these various contexts the potential and, at times, actual danger of police work blends with the hedonism which the lower ranks expect in their work. They do not want to get hurt and are often as frightened as anyone else when danger is present; it would be stupid to suggest otherwise. Yet the fun that is found in many potentially dangerous situations can be exploited to sustain the action of 'real' police work.

Terms like 'police violence' and 'police brutality' tend to distort the distasteful but, to the officers concerned, sophisticated means of using force. Their grammar of force relates particular tactics to particular prisoners and offences. Further, terms like 'violence' and 'brutality' conceal the related but distinct nuances of different forms of force. The more symbolic aspects of force, which frequently fuse with the instrumental aim of obtaining a confession of guilt, have been discussed in considerable detail. During the questioning of a suspect the power of the police is both symbolized and realized. Indeed, when an officer has been assaulted this power, which is given by the state and exploited by the rank and file, is reasserted to sustain police authority.

However, we should not suppose that physical force is used only to achieve the instrumentalist purposes of the state; it is also used to enhance features of policing which may well be somewhat peripheral to its objective conditions. Action and hedonism are two such features; they are not 'icing on the cake' but central to what the rank and file recognizes as real police work. The situations in which it is possible to use force – when authority is challenged, officers are assaulted, danger is present – are the raw material by which the occupational culture is verified, affirmed and sustained. Stories of how so-and-so hit so-and-so live on. They become legend, providing entertainment which only a sociologist like me could call the 'social construction' of policing.

10

Sustaining the Occupational Culture

As various aspects of police work have been considered, the possibility has been mooted that officers could understand and deal with incidents in a different fashion. Action and excitement, the control of space and persons held in custody, the use of force and the extraction of confessions need not be their primary concerns. These are highly selective aspects of their work. Policing at Hilton is constructed by the lower ranks – which means not that it is concocted out of thin air but that the various legal and policy instruments available to the staff are modified as the rules in the book are translated into rules in use of the ground.

This idea of policing as a 'social construction' is not new; Peter Manning (1977, p. 80; 1980) has written about it at length. However, as far as research into British policing is concerned, the idea has hardly developed beyond the speculations of theory. Although many different means of sustaining the occupational culture have already been outlined, just two of the ways in which Hilton's officers construct and preserve their idea of what constitutes routine police work will be considered to underpin this theoretical perspective with some illustrative data. The first, which is the manner in which cars and radio communication are used, is perhaps not as central as the second, the making and sustaining of police folk narratives.

Unit beat policing – cars and radios

Wholesale schemes of unit beat policing, like that found at Hilton, have now been adapted or replaced by a variety of policies called 'community policing' (Alderson, 1979; Moore and Brown,

1981). Policemen know that old ideas die hard, and the assumptions underpinning the use to which Panda cars and radios have been put will not disappear without trace; being an 'asphalt cowboy' (Punch, 1979a) is much more fun than working as a community constable. But the view of the home-beat constables who walk their own beat is that:

> The blokes here just don't know how to walk a beat. They never get out and meet anybody. They don't know how to talk to anybody. I think it's terrible. There is a proper way to walk a beat, you know, but do they know? No, they don't. They want to ride around in Panda cars, and they don't want to get out and walk around and meet people and talk to people. They just haven't got a clue.

And they are right – their colleagues rarely want to walk a beat; they are not lazy but simply believe that vehicles are essential for routine policing.

Cars allow PCs to concentrate on 'getting work', which generally means arrests. When an officer who should be walking a beat is seen riding in one of the Pandas he is asked for an explanation. He replies: 'For work, sarge, to get more work. I've checked around by beat and it is OK, so I am trying to get some work.' A young probationer constable is posted by his sergeant to the night-duty crime car. The driver is told: ' – is your crew for the second half, and for God's sake get him an arrest. He hasn't had any this month.' So cars are seen as a means of getting what is considered to be work, despite the fact that for years they were not used at all for general patrol. They have been built into the young officer's assumptions about how to patrol and what constitutes effective work. If patrolling in a vehicle is a primary interest, emergencies and crime work are at a premium; these priorities are the shared, commonsense ideas of the lower ranks that will not disappear overnight.

Cars can also create and sustain the action and excitement that PCs expect from their work. When a patrol car reports over the personal or force radio that it is chasing a stolen vehicle, it is quite usual for other drivers to join in, even though they are formally prohibited from doing so and will probably make what is already a fairly dangerous situation even more precarious. At one time this problem became so serious – the accidents that occurred during chases and the long processions of police cars with lights flashing and horns sounding become embarrassing – that the force published an official order in an attempt to control things. The order was read to the PCs on parade. Reactions varied:

'Oh, it doesn't affect me much.'

'They might as well write that on the wall. Let's be honest, they might as well do that.'

'But if R/T [receiver/transmitter] drivers have no bottle, then they'll get away from us. "Keep a reasonable distance", that's stupid. If you've got an old PC trained twenty years ago and he's got no bottle, then you've got to have somebody chase and to get it.'

A sergeant asked this officer, 'Well, would you try and overtake an R/T car if you were in a Panda or something?'

PC: 'No.'

Sergeant: 'All this parading around in rows of cars is stupid. All you need is one or two cars chasing.'

PC: 'Yes, but some drivers won't go after them, will they?'

The inspector agrees with the sergeant and says, 'It's not right that you should be chasing people around just to get the thrill.'

PC: 'Yes, but it's fun, isn't it?'

The officers who had been listening laughed.

After several patrolling officers speed to the scene of a suspected break-in, one of Hilton's constables notices a colleague's late arrival. He shouts, 'Last again! Last again! Where have you been?' When the police use of time is discussed, a simulated chase between a sergeant and constable is described; when a colleague drives at high speed to an incident he says it is 'fun'; when officers give accounts of a chase in which they have been involved it seems that they tried to provoke a stolen vehicle to 'go for it' rather than stop the vehicle immediately. Fast driving constitutes action and excitement. The vehicles used in unit beat policing are driven not only to respond to calls from members of the public, to provide a visible police presence in Hilton and to transport officers but also to construct and sustain this sense of policing as action and challenge.

Personal radios are also adapted to these ends. All officers carry personal radios when they patrol; the 'talk-through' facility means that each officer can hear all transmissions made in the subdivision, and during each shift of eight hours a great deal of information is passed from officer to officer, as well as from Hilton police station to individual officers. A PC who wants help can request it over his radio; if a message to a car is made over the separate 999 system, the crew can broadcast it throughout the subdivision on the personal radio network. However, these formal arrangements are adapted to the requirements of the lower ranks. There is a tendency for all calls which sound exciting to be broadcast to the officers in cars and on foot. Requests for help are made whenever an incident looks as if it could get out of hand, however unlikely that eventuality may be.

On one occasion I was station officer during a late shift. The communications officers, including a civilian telephonist who had worked at Hilton for many years, were in my office. A call was broadcast from the 999 car to all PCs, via the PR system: 'All units Hilton, call to outside –. Woman being assaulted.'

From my previous knowledge of police work I could find no reason for this broadcast and thought the incident trivial, expecting it to be over by the time any vehicles arrived at the location. There would soon be another call to turn units away. I said to a constable who was in the office, 'How the hell did policemen manage when they were without cars and radios? It's crazy asking people to go on such a call.'

The PC replied: 'So you would prefer to see a policeman get a hiding would you, sarge?'

I replied, 'No, but he won't get a hiding, will he? All these technical aids make for bad policing.'

He said, 'Well, there wasn't the crime before we had them.'

The telephonist who had been listening butted in: 'No, but policemen had just as much to do and they didn't get assaulted.'

At this point another message was broadcast calling other units to cancel.

Following an incident during which a PC hit a coloured youth with his truncheon, another telephonist who had also worked at the station for a considerable number of years made the following comments to me. Since the old personal radios came in, I think that instead of talking their way out of trouble like the old coppers did and getting by that way, they just pull their truncheons out and shout for assistance on the PR. They don't talk their way out of it at all. They just ask for assistance and get their truncheons out.

Radios and cars were used very selectively in these incidents, and certainly not in line with official policy. The equipment of unit beat policing is adapted to suit the preference of lower ranks; as this happens, the occupational culture is maintained and strengthened.

Folk narratives – keeping the tradition alive

Popular policemen can spin a good yarn; they can hold their own in the canteen, billiard room or station office at three in the morning with a 'goodly one' about a chase and fight. The finale is generally a description, in fine detail, of the last sociologist who tried to research them. Sociologists who survive their experience of research remember these stories but tend to save them up for bar chat at conferences. They provide superb entertainment and repel the grasping hand of analysis.

The jokes and stories told about policing at Hilton are certainly entertaining; there is also much more to them. This rich mixture of narrative preserves the traditions of the occupational culture, sustaining it against the odds of experience. More formally, and as a good deal of the sociological literature on humour and joking suggests, narrative releases some of the tensions and makes sense of the contradictions of police work (Coser, 1959, 1960; Roy, 1960; Zijderfeld, 1968).

If you listen carefully to PC 123 holding forth during a game of cards, you will hear how his values and strategies of policing are pitted against alternative and more authoritative definitions of policing, which can constrain him and his colleagues. When policemen tell jokes and stories to each other they are sustaining their definition of policing as *the* practical, commonsense way of working. That definition is compared with, and triumphs over, other potentially more cogent definitions framed by senior officers, the law, courts and the range of people with an interest in police work. The police folk narrative therefore mediates different levels of organizational structure (Douglas, 1975). It exposes the reality of policing – the adaptations to the formal structure made by the lower ranks – and affirms its supremacy. Although the stories told are frequently exaggerated, highly dramatic and probably inaccurate, their power is considerable. When the relief gathers in the station office for the night-duty tea break, something more than a 'policeman's Jackanory' is taking place, as Hannerz (1969, p. 111) points out:

> definitions and evaluations of self, others and the external world are developed, maintained and displayed with greater intensity than in other interaction. . . . An individual's vision of reality is often a precarious thing; we can find comfort in the knowledge that it is shared by others, thus acquiring social anchoring in an objective truth.

Team discipline

Policing at Hilton requires teamwork involving a measure of discipline and loyalty among the ranks which cannot always be guaranteed. We have noted the problems of being overheard in the station office and the fact that an inspector has to ensure that police information is not exchanged in public hearing. Teams are tenuous groupings, and in some narratives, many of which are humorous, stress is placed on the implications of team membership for various ranks and the consequences of breaching discipline. A number of stories are concerned with the initiation of recruits into team membership; a constable tells one to the relief during the 4.30 a.m. tea break:

> A PC had recently arrived at Hilton and was required to ride a cycle around an obstacle course in the station yard. We told him it was a test to see if he could ride a cycle in the force. We awarded him a certificate, 'Cyclists Union of National Transport' and down the side of the certificate were letters CUNT, in Gothic lettering. He showed it

to his father, who was an ex-Chief Superintendent, who
realized it and didn't think it was so funny.

This is followed by a story of another officer who has to complete
a rather different test when he arrives at Hilton. He rides up a
ramp towards an open window and has to negotiate various
obstacles. On another occasion he is told that there are suspects
on an island in the middle of a lake; needless to say, the story has
a punch line about how he runs through the water to get to them.
The sequence of stories about initiation end with one about a PC
who is asked to check all the Belisha beacons in a particular road
to see if they are flashing in sequence. If they are not, he has to
decide which lamp is irregular and record its serial number,
printed on the underside of the bulb, which means that he has to
climb the pole of the beacon. The whole relief watches as he does
all this.

These narratives, though humorous and entertaining to the
officers who form the audience, emphasize that the new recruit is
a member of a team and, indeed, that his colleagues have some
power over him. Particular obligations follow from membership,
not least when a colleague falls foul of discipline regulations
or appears to have broken the law. On one occasion an officer
has been arrested by a colleague for driving with too much
alcohol in his blood stream. After relating the tale a supervisory officer affirms that no grudge is borne by the officer under
arrest: 'I know he holds no malice against you. He doesn't hold
anything against you at all.' Loyalty to the occupation and
especially to the team of colleagues is pitted against the requirements of the law. The solidarity of the team is threatened, but
membership and interdependency remain in tact.

When PCs break force regulations, their supervisors often
have to offer support because the offence also makes them
vulnerable to a charge of inadequate supervision. Sergeants and
inspectors are therefore part of the team but also have to try to
keep their distance in case they have to book a PC. Supervisors
are reminded of this relationship by stories about how they have
offered support when mistakes have been made in the past. A
prisoner has been in hospital under police guard. He goes to the
toilet and escapes through a window and down a drainpipe. The
constable has to think quickly and is backed up by his supervisory officer when he explains that he gave chase but slipped on

a wet floor that had recently been cleaned. The story is told when the officers involved are listening, together with an inspector and two more PCs. One of these PCs, who was on duty at the time, says:

> 'He let him go. He lost him. We told a lot of lies about that, didn't we? I mean, to get you off. I was supervising traffic points at the time.' All the officers laugh or smile.

Of course, there are times when an officer's action causes the team to fragment, and the damage done cannot be repaired quickly. A sergeant finds a dispute difficult to manage after the inspector has 'assisted' him:

> I had them all quietened down and was listening to what they were telling me. But she'll only listen to one side of the story, that's all she'll do. She came in, she heard somebody who either looked the most respectable or somebody who's crying. She'll go up to them and listen to them and she just creates havoc and then pisses off. Well, that's bloody hopeless.

A similar theme is expounded when a sergeant tells his colleagues, about a court hearing.

> Did you hear about the job at – [names another station] ? This is the honest truth. Two PCs at – nicked a ponce, and they were giving their evidence about two toms with a customer. They call a defence witness, and who should walk into the court but PC –, and he says that the tom couldn't have been where the police officer said she was because she was in bed with him. He was transferred the same day.

The police team, then, provides an interdependent structure of relationships which are supportive and, in part, capable of keeping indiscipline within bounds. These narratives affirm the identity of the team and the obligations of membership and provide some information about how to deal with its potential breakdown.

Although the PCs do not worry too much about the accuracy of their stories, some narratives can stretch credibility too far, prompting a revision in which a greater measure of the truth is revealed. As an officer recalls a cat-and-mouse chase with a car driven by a drunk, he stresses that he went backwards and forwards along the road, making fun of the inspector, who apparently made no effort to get out of the police car to stop the drunken driver. However, the inspector is none too pleased with the criticism levelled at him and suggests that the account of the chase is more fictional than real:

> 'If you're not careful, I'll tell the true story. I'll tell the truth.'
>   SH: 'What's this?'
>   The police driver said, 'I'm not worried. It doesn't worry me.'
>   His critic then ended the exchange, 'Yes, I'd watch it because I'll tell the truth.' Laughter.

To an outsider, the humour of many of these narratives may seem limp or incomprehensible. From the insiders' perspective the humour of many of the stories acts to release some of the tension between the way in which the rank-and-file officers work and the various constraints under which that work takes place. Humour seems to make these tensions explicit and public, then closes the breach through an appreciation of the teamwork of the lower ranks and the need to sustain co-operation. 'Normal policing' continues and is strengthened.

The relief – roles and rank

Different styles of policemanship will be found in any team. The focus on central features of the occupational culture in this study inevitably glosses over these differences in order to describe the dominant style, against which variations are assessed (Chatterton, 1981). Nevertheless, officers who, for one reason or another deviate from the dominant style can become the subject of stories and humour, which highlight their excesses or apparent weaknesses.

A probationer constable who works in a very restrained manner – he does not force himself on people or find the action of policework particularly attractive – is teased by a colleague:

There's something wrong with – [name] tonight, you know. There's definitely something wrong with him. He told somebody to 'fuck off' today. Then we had this 'suspect shout', and he's running along beside this bloke he knows, asking him when he's going out for a drink, and there could have been this PC getting his head kicked in some way down the road. There's something wrong with – [name].

On another occasion a sergeant sends him up:

'Have you been beating up prisoners, then?'
    Another officer: 'Yes, he has. I wouldn't mind so long as he didn't leave them paralysed in the corner of the detention room. Do you know what he [the suspect] did to – [officer]? He pulled his tie off. Just flicked it off when he went to speak to him.'
    Other sergeant: 'Didn't that annoy you?'
    PC: 'Not really, sarge.'
    PS: 'Well, don't hit him then.'

Humour marks out the boundaries of the occupational culture and so places this constable within the broad and vivid context of police work as his colleagues think it should be performed (Reed *et al.*, 1977).
    Attempts to limit the excesses of a highly excitable officer, who rushes to any incident and constantly expects to be involved in fights, are similarly framed by humorous narratives. He frequently uses the personal radio to ask colleagues to stop vehicles which he thinks are stolen and, although he rarely, if ever, makes an arrest, always demands the utmost emergency. The relief is weary of this, and on one occasion the reply is: 'Is this a real chase or a "Smith" chase?', which adds to his reputation, outlined more clearly in a story told during an early morning tea break, when the whole relief is present. A PC begins, making his first point to the inspector:

You weren't here when it happened, but it's the funniest thing I've heard. Old – [names officer] was sitting on the pan out there one night duty when he heard a chase coming down – [road in which station is situated]. So he hoists his trousers up, and the next thing we see he's standing in the

High Road with his truncheon in his hand holding his
trousers with his other hand. The car hadn't come down – .
It had turned off somewhere. When we asked him, he said,
'Well, I thought they were going to come down here and I
was going to throw my stick at the windscreen.' He had his
shirt on, no epaulettes, his trousers weren't done up and his
shirt tails were flapping and he had his stick in his hand. He
was ready to throw the stick at the car.

Like his colleague who is considered too passive, this excitable
PC is the subject of a humorous tale which circumscribes his
behaviour within the limits of the relief's tolerance.

A protest against unacceptable behaviour is equally obvious
when a cartoon is drawn on the door of one of the toilets. It
pictures a PC whose reputation for using violence is considerable (several complaints about his behaviour are being investigated). The cartoon pictures him with a swastika on his fore-
head; his name and the words 'Obturbanführer – is a wanker. Ya
Vohl!' are printed underneath. Someone adds a gun in one hand,
a truncheon in the other and the caption: 'Did you say that kid
stole some Smarties? Let me sort him out.'

Although supervisory ranks are drawn into the team, some
distinction of rank is, and has to be, clearly recognized. The
sergeants and inspectors have to work closely with the PCs who,
we know, are not slow to recall their superiors' failings. The
routine and acceptable method by which the PCs acknowledge
the relationship involves a measure of sarcasm

A constable asks an inspector, 'Would you get me a meal,
sir?' [This entails a walk to the local chip shop.]
Inspector: 'I see.'
PC: 'I'm always getting them for you, sir.'

When a constable uses the radio to ask a sergeant to go to a
particular address he gets the reply:

'No, I'm over at West Street at the moment. Get somebody else to
do it.'
This place is a long way off Hilton's ground, and another
constable breaks in on behalf of his colleague: ' – [names first
constable] wants to know what you are doing at West Street.'

Sergeant: 'I want to know what – is doing at the station. He can go and check the premises.'

When a sergeant is posted to the station and is seen patrolling with another sergeant who has a reputation for verballing, a constable asks,

'Are you patrolling with the new sergeant? Teaching him to bend the evidence. "Sergeant – the swifter", teaching him to give bent evidence.'

All of these conversations draw laughter from the PCs because they remind supervisors that the lower ranks have information about them, which restricts their disciplinary role and so tempers the authority of their rank. Tension between the ranks is informally acknowledged and defused within the framework of the PCs assumptions.

Discipline reports are very infrequent, but stories about how senior officers are defeated when they try to discipline PCs are told with a flourish of triumph, as was the case with this one, which the PC in question loved to tell. He liked to wear a scarf under his uniform mackintosh, which at one time was contrary to regulations. Despite several cautions from a senior officer, he continued to wear the scarf and was eventually formally 'booked'. However, before the disciplinary hearing was held he got a note from a doctor verifying that he had to wear the scarf for medical reasons. The senior officer was defeated. Another constable talks about a similar victory:

PC: 'Wouldn't it be nice to see him going over a red light just after he had retired?'
Colleague: 'Or because he had retired.'
PC: 'I was in a bank . . . on one occasion and we had a superintendent, – [name], here. He had left the job but he came into the bank, and yours truly was standing at the counter. He told me that he hoped he wouldn't be there too long because he had his car outside on a yellow line. I said, "Look, guv'nor, your car is on a yellow line there and you'll get a ticket, no bother." So he's straight out of the bank and moving it.'

During a quiet Sunday afternoon shift several officers exchange stories about challenges that lower ranks have offered to their superiors. One PC recalls that when he worked at another station a sergeant retired from the force but refused to move out of his police house. Senior officers made many attempts to persuade him to leave the house, but he continually defied them; he was determined to move only when the local council evicted him. A challenge like this is reckoned to level the authority of senior officers – it is a gentle reminder that they can be 'had over' by the very officers whom they try to supervise.

Another story followed directly. An officer who had recently retired was suspected of an offence. Senior officers interviewed him and asked him to go to the station. He refused; if they wanted him at the nick, they could arrest him there and then. He knew that they had insufficient evidence to do that, and the inquiry had to be abandoned. The officers listening found this tale, like the others, extremely amusing, not least because of the successful challenge made to senior officers. In each narrative the rank-and-file definition of police work remains intact, despite the attempts of senior officers to enforce discipline; indeed, the joyous triumph experienced in the telling of each story strengthens and sustains the lower ranks' perspective.

Action

Contrary to what you may have gleaned from *Sweeney* and *Operation Carter*, police work is really a very quiet occupation (Morris and Heal, 1981, pp. 9–28). Long periods of walking around and waiting are interspersed with occasional incidents, usually mundane. This reality does not match the popular image of a world pulsating with action and excitement. It is interesting that these narratives often unfold at the quietest times, like the early-morning tea break and on Sunday, when little is happening. Perhaps the experience of working in a quiet job is then more threatening than at any other time?

'Bandit drivers' – those who give chase in a stolen car – are respected:

He was a pretty good driver and he had his wrist in plaster when he finished as well. He was pretty good. He didn't hit any cars on the way round and he didn't have any crashes at all. So he did pretty well.

'Bandits' provide that challenge to police control and action which takes precedence over other aspects of work and erodes the attempts of senior officers to stop the PCs from chasing around. The force order which prohibits all but advanced drivers from joining in car chases is put to the test soon after its publication, when a chase takes place near Hilton and prompts some wry remarks:

> PC: 'Oh yes, he put up a good fight.'
> SH: 'Well, did he stop of his own accord?'
> PC: 'No, only because a couple of cars were put across the road and he didn't have much choice. Mind you, there were lots of cars there, all chasing him.'
> Other PC: 'Yes, there were cars everywhere, sarge.'
> PC: 'Yes, that police order really went down well.'
> [Laughter]

Characteristically, in this exchange the controls which can be applied to the lower ranks are juxtaposed with the way in which the lads work and with their expectations. They call the television programme *The Sweeney* their 'instruction class', and to judge from their reaction to the police order, it seems that Inspector Regan has the edge over their own senior officers.

A love of speed is closely related to the cultivation of drama in accounts of police work. Trivial offences can be recounted in almost spectacular terms. A few days after officers arrest a number of juveniles for causing a slight disturbance in the street but end up without any prosecutions, the incident is described as 'an affray', which is one of the most serious public order offences and an inappropriate description of what happened. Quiet times are dramatically contrasted with the constant likelihood of being really busy:

> Yes, you can think it's quiet, but I can tell you, if you were station officer on a Bank Holiday like – [names officer] was, and you expect nothing to happen and you have eighteen prisoners by midnight, then that's how this station goes. It was an affray. – was the duty officer and – [names suspect]

was in here, and he'd already been pushed up against the
wall by yours truly. Then Sergeant – walks in with a gun. It
was a shotgun they'd fired into a pub. He went up to [the
suspect] and said, 'Who had the gun?' and smashed him
straight round the face, and the bloke went up the wall and
up the ceiling. [Laughter]

After a potentially serious disturbance at a club catering for black
youths, officers return to Hilton and recount what has happened,
stressing the danger of the situation and the smart way in which
they have dealt with it. The dog handler walks in; his dog is
carrying a knitted hat, the type worn by many black youths.

The inspector asked, 'Is that the war trophy? Good boy.'
PC: 'Yes, we brought it especially for you.'
Inspector: 'It is necessary to use dogs for the coloureds
because they're so bloody violent and that's why you want
them. I can tell you I was at – [names scene of violent
demonstration] when we had the horses, and I can tell you
we were really pleased to see them.'
Other stories of similar incidents followed.

Along with other stories and humorous interjections in conversation, drama, exaggeration and evocation are used to link
events which have little or nothing to do with each other. Hilton's
world of fast-moving fun, of challenge and action, is constructed
and maintained. But don't forget: this world hardly exists –
which is why a story at tea break is vital.

Questioning of suspects

One of the areas of police work where some officers sail close to
the wind is the questioning of prisoners. The very clear separation between certain 'working practices' and the requirements of
formal policy and law provides material for humour and narrative.

After his annual appraisal interview with the Chief Superintendent, a constable returns to duty in the station. A
colleague asks: 'How did you get on?'

PC: 'Fine, fine. "Enthusiastic" I am, you know.' Both officers laugh.

Colleague: 'Yes, really enthusiastic.'

Officer interviewed: 'Professional ability, nil. Appearance, nil, grotesque. Yes, but he can't half hit prisoners.' Both laugh.

On another occasion a sergeant is talking to the inspector in charge of his relief, and he mentions a notice advertising the annual force boxing tournament. Making reference to the name of the cup presented to the winner of the tournament, the 'Crown Cup', the inspector asks his sergeant: 'You haven't amended this notice yet?'

'What notice, sir?'

'The "Brown Cup". No, every time I get a drunk in I tell him to hit him, but he won't do it.' Both laugh.

('Brown' is the name of an officer who is developing a reputation for using force on prisoners.) Other tales are also concerned with occasions when force has been used.

PC: 'But who would have known that you could have seen – [names suspect] from this very canteen?'

Another PC: 'Well, I must say I'm one of the few officers, the only officer at this station who was able to see – [suspect] on the day he was nicked.'

First PC: 'No, you weren't. I was one of the eight who carried him down the cell passage and threw him into a cell. Was he in a fuckin' state? I can tell you he really was, but he didn't get a doctor. Old – [names very senior officer on division] came in and said, "Don't you need a doctor for that man?" I said, "Who needs a doctor? What man? What state?" Believe me, he was in a hell of a state. His face was terrible.'

Other PC: 'Yes, – [names colleague] was gaoler on that day and he tells the same story.'

Incidents are not always as spectacular as this one, but many nonetheless generate anecdotes about the people concerned and the consequences for officers when force is used on prisoners. First, part of a story about an officer:

He was very fat and used to nudge a prisoner with his belly.
He'd have a constable with him who would say, 'Answer
when the sergeant speaks to you.' The prisoners would be
nudged all around the charge room. [Laughter]

This next account, told with great style at 4 a.m., stresses the use
of force and the excitement it generates:

'I've decided that you bring me all the grief.'
  'I don't bring you the grief.'
  'Oh yes, I was the one who held the poor man's arm up his
back and stamped on his cigar, because you aren't allowed
to smoke in the food department of the store.'
  Colleague, using West Indian accent: 'But then it was
the little one who held me.' Laughter.

After two officers arrest a prisoner who has put up a considerable
fight, one notices that the other has been bitten on the neck.

The injured officer says, 'A coon gave me a love bite on the
neck.'
  As the prisoner lay on the floor of the charge room with
blood oozing from his wound, a constable referred to his
groaning with wry humour. 'We don't allow singing.'
  After the injured officer had received hospital treatment,
the night-duty staff arrived for duty. One of them asked,
'Who gave you a love bite, then? What happened to you?
Don't forget criminal injuries.'

An officer tells colleagues about the use of force in public at a
football match:

I was there with – [names officer] leaning on a support. A
teenager told – [officer] that he'd been leaning on the support and he wanted it back. – [the officer] went *wham*.
[Laughs] Did he give him a thump, and this kid went
tumbling down.

The 'rules' governing the use of force can be neglected:

I hit one of them before I realized he was intelligent. I went

the wrong way there. It would have been better to talk to
him, but I thought he was thick when I first stopped him.

All of these anecdotes point to the relationship between forbidden police practices and the limits prescribed by law and
policy. The tension between the two is exposed and handled;
humour is a cocoon within which safety can be found and
a satisfactory, if temporary, resolution identified. There is
another aspect to consider: if one function of humour and narrative is to sustain the occupational culture, another is the provision of an acceptable medium through which to express and
acknowledge danger, nervousness and fear about some facets of
police work. These are emotions that should not normally be
expressed among colleagues – they are largely forbidden, save
within this safe context.

The use of force is not the only strategy that entails a risk of
discipline or worse. Verballing is handled similarly in stories.
After a court case:

> First colleague: 'Did you win then?'
> PC involved in the case: 'No, we lost!'
> Second colleague: 'It's not a matter of winning or losing.
> Justice was seen to be done.'
> PC: 'Despite what I said.'
> Second colleague: 'Yes, despite my verbals justice was
> done.' Laughs.

Again, the forbidden but now regularized underworld of policing
is laid bare. Verballing may require a rehearsal in the station to
make sure that a challenge from a defence lawyer in court can be
met:

> PC: 'He [a defence witness] couldn't have heard what –
> [arresting officer] was saying to that bloke. I could see him
> from some way off, and I know that from where he was, he
> couldn't have heard him.'
> Sergeant: 'Well, officer, how do you know he couldn't
> hear? If you were some distance away, it's quite impossible
> for you to say that.'
> PC: 'No it is not. I could see him quite clearly, and I
> know in that crowd he couldn't hear what – was saying.'

> Sergeant: 'Come along, officer, you're changing your story now. You know you can't say that at all, and you're changing your story.'
> PC: 'The black nigger bastard.'

On another occasion two officers are recording their evidence in connection with an arrest:

> PC: 'I've got more in my book than you.' Laughter.
> The other officer holds up blank pages in his own book and says: 'Well, have you got the verbals?'
> PC listening: 'I don't think I should be hearing this.' Laughter again.
> PC: 'Officer, when did you make these notes?'
> Other officer: 'At the time, sir.' Laughter.

Just as the use of force is normalized, so the manipulation of the rules for preparing and presenting evidence is placed within the comparative safety of the narrative. Dangers remain, and the extreme case can sound a warning for all officers:

> I knew a CID sergeant who had fitted a bloke up with an indecent exposure. They just stopped him as he walked around a corner and gave it to him. After the hearing this prisoner hung himself and now the DS is a wreck. He's had a mental breakdown and will never be the same again.

The population policed

As we have noted, 'challengers' are able to threaten the way in which the police work. At the station lawyers may ruin the questioning of a suspect, and if they cross-examine a police witness in court, it is possible that the police work done in the privacy of the station will be exposed in public. It is no surprise, then, that the tensions provoked by lawyers are released in the telling of jokes and anecdotes.

> He [the barrister] stood up, and before he said anything the beak said, 'Can I tell you that you've got a hard job on? You're really wasting your time.' So he let him go on a bit and then told him to sit down because he had heard enough.

The barrister said that he had never been talked to like this before and never been told that he couldn't complete his pleading.

The beak asked the usher for the Law Society's list and asked the barrister if he was on it. It was the 1972 list and he looked it through. Well, this bloke wasn't on it, and so the beak says, 'I remand this case for a week to find out if you are qualified.'

You should have seen the bastard's face, poor sod. It just finished him.

In a rather different context – a solicitor employed by the force is talking to some sergeants – a deliberate slip of the tongue gets a laugh. A sergeant begins a question: 'When a defendant has got a mouthpiece – sorry, I mean solicitor. . . .'

Similar themes run through stories about social workers, who are reckoned to be easily 'had over' by 'villains' and even by juvenile offenders.

'One of the social workers was the custody officer. She had five young coloured kids in there who had been done for "dipping". So she had her handbag on the table, didn't see? Of course she had her purse nicked. Well, she couldn't understand this; couldn't make it out. We got the money back for her in the end, but there you are, she left her bloody handbag on the table. Bloody marvellous, isn't it?'

Other similar stories followed, and the sequence was ended by an officer who said: 'Yes, it's frightening, isn't it, when you see some of these social workers who are supposed to look after these kids, frightening.'

Finally, blacks are frequently the subject of humour, not least because they allege discriminatory treatment.

A constable noticed a black youth talking to a white girl while standing in a queue. Both were waiting to go into a public building, controlled by the police. The officer on duty at the door of the building stopped him and the officer watching observed, 'Why are you arresting me, officer? One law for the black man and one for the white man.'

As officers from Hilton passed through an area of black settlement on their way to a special function, one used a West Indian accent and joked, 'Look at that honky-tonk black man with his beret with a bobble on. What a lovely man he is with that bobble-hat on. Oh, this is West Indian area, this is where we all live. The policeman is telling lies in court. He is not telling the truth.'

All of these anecdotes, stories and jokes feed and sustain the occupational culture because they stand between the officers and groups in Hilton who can try to call them to account. They may be true; they may sometimes be false. Accuracy is not the point of narrative, which selects and reifies particular experiences of policing at Hilton to sustain the world of the lower ranks.

There narratives echo what research into policing has hinted at but not yet documented. Mary Douglas's (1975) comments on joking have a wider application when she suggests, first, that this form of communication juxtaposes control with that which is controlled and, secondly, that the juxtaposition dictates the triumph of that which is controlled. This is exactly what occurs in these police narratives. They deal with various aspects of the occupational culture, exposing them in a safe setting, putting them against alternative understandings of police work and then closing the breach in such a way that the lower ranks perspective survives and usually triumphs.

This 'social construction of policing' is never wholly complete. The risks of discipline for PCs and ranked colleagues always remain; the danger and 'dirty work' of the occupation never become palatable. And this ensures the importance and continuation of the oral tradition. In sharing some of this tradition of policing at Hilton we have stepped a little further inside a police world which is precarious and in need of support. The tales, allegedly based on personal experience, may seem trite and at times fantastic – just talk between policemen. But such talk is essential if their world is to retain any semblance of order.

11

A Professional Police Force

Description, analysis and prescription are rarely, if ever separable; research into the work of the police is informed by hope of change, sometimes dormant, sometimes active. Such commitment does not pre-empt impartiality. Without some appreciation of the fact that sociological research is concerned with real lives and, ultimately, with the question of what it means to be human, its bland statistical and theoretical monuments would all too easily be beatified and 'isms' would provide a haven of distortions. It is important for a reader to discern where value misleads, theory controls, prescription meets evidence. A writer should facilitate discernment as far as possible, constantly aware of the tendency to create in his own human image. Nevertheless, the requirements of scholarship oblige him tentatively to bridge thought and action, analysis and policy.

The riots in some British cities during 1981 drew public attention to the police. As the opening paragraphs of this book suggest, many constabularies are reviewing their policies; more academics than ever are writing about the police; criticisms abound. These contemporary and particular factors combine with the more general commitments of research to press for some consideration of the relevance of Hilton's police to future policy. In order to address these policy issues, it is necessary to return to the historical setting of the research itself.

The aims and effects of professionalization

> I suppose you could sum it all up by saying that in Britain
> certainly, and I have no doubt elsewhere, the time has come
> when the police are abandoning their artisan status and are
> achieving, by our ever-increasing variety of services, our
> integrity, our accountability and our dedication to the
> public good, a status no less admirable than that of the most
> learned and distinguished professions. The constable of
> 1829 and 1929 would have regarded that objective as a
> dream unattainable as the climbing of Everest. For the
> constable of 1975 it is clearly a visible peak which he is
> rapidly climbing. (Mark, 1977, p. 42)

Robert Mark summarizes some major themes of policing during
the late 1960s and early 1970s. By the time that my fieldwork at
Hilton began, the force's chief and its senior officers were openly
regarding themselves as members of a profession (Holdaway,
1977). The notion of 'professional policing' still finds a place in a
variety of policies and practices, all of which are represented at
Hilton and have a bearing on the work of the lower ranks.

During the early 1960s an important basis of police status and
authority was diminishing. Many senior officers who had joined
the police force after serving as officers in the armed forces were
retiring: the scheme by which they had entered the police at
officer rank had been abandoned; all recruits now joined as
constables. These new recruits lacked the educational qualifications of their superior officers and offered few other skills on
which a new competency could be built. The Royal Commission
on the Police, which finally reported in 1962, drew attention to
the issue of the public accountability of the police, sensitizing
chief officers and the Home Office to the questioning of public
authority. A number of criminal trials which received national
publicity – particularly the revelations of malpractice and violence during the interrogation of some suspects by the Sheffield
CID (Home Office, 1963), and the case of Detective Sergeant
Challenor (Home Office, 1965), charged with perjury and conspiracy to pervert the course of justice – cast doubt on the accountability and methods of policing. If the supposed rigidity of
police discipline could not be assured by quasi-military styles of

command, where might an alternative base of internal control be found?

At this very time, just as police status and authority were being called into question, the police found themselves increasingly required to liaise with, for example, social service agencies, traffic departments and community relations officers. On the whole, the representatives of these and other public agencies had professional status and were legitimately concerned with matters of direct relevance to police policy and decision-making. As the old basis of police status and authority was eroded, so new foundations for parity with the representatives of these agencies and a more secure public image had to be laid. This parity was deemed to be located in the notion of a 'professional police'.

No longer would police competence be based on ill-defined 'common sense'. With the aid of the resources of what was then called the National Police College at Bramshill, now the Police Staff College, the expertise of the few serving graduate officers and a revised basic training for recruits, a body of knowledge drawn from a range of academic disciplines was applied to operational policing. Although it was never formally collated in a single text, this body of knowledge embraced both law enforcement and peacekeeping aspects of policing, recognizing their equality (Stead, 1973).

The development of a diverse corpus of knowledge prompted greater specialization in the service. Police specialists in traffic management, computerization, communications, community relations – the list is extensive – could now use their particular knowledge to liaise with those doing similar work in central and local government. Technology is of importance here because as it was, and continues to be, employed in the traffic control, data collection and patrol spheres of police work; an appearance of competence and professional status was enhanced.

Specialist knowledge and technological innovation were further associated in the context of police discretion. Senior officers – Mark was probably the first – began to articulate the view that errors like those highlighted in the Sheffield and Challenor cases would, as far as possible, be controlled with rigour. Corrupt officers would be purged from the police service; the rule of law would receive due regard. Bad law, however, would be exposed, and the police would lobby for reform of the law.

The police alone see the whole crime reported to them, most of which never reaches a court and they are no longer the semi-literate, unthinking mercenaries of long ago. No discussion of criminal justice can be complete without their participation, far too long delayed. (Mark, 1977, p. 261)

Particular attention was paid to the arrest and questioning of a suspect. The 'professional method' emphasized the slow accumulation of evidence, if necessary with the support of specialist and technical aids to provide evidence of guilt before rather than after arrest. Law was henceforth to be invoked within a framework of 'informed discretion'.

We decided that it would be worthwhile to discover everything we could about [criminals'] movements, their associates, and their weaknesses simply as an insurance against the probability that they would commit further crimes. Thus the description 'target criminals'. (ibid., p. 312)

If the consequence of working in this way within the rule of law led to the acquittal of guilty persons, so be it; but no one should expect the police to retire from public debate and to cease pressing for reform (Chibnall, 1977; Reiner, 1980).

While attention was paid to crime, the police also recognized that many of the problems with which they dealt were social problems. Officers of all ranks now make judgements about such matters and display a professional competence which matches that of social workers and probation officers. The police, it is argued,

are what might be described as social diagnosticians. Their role is to recognize social crises or their incipient causes and to activate other social agencies where expertise is needed. As yet the formalization of the role of social diagnostician has not been fully developed but it is in this field that the police should be expected to continue to operate. In a society where social welfare services are rapidly developing the police should seek to help more in the field. (Alderson, 1973, p. 45)

The implication of these ideas about knowledge and 'informed discretion' is that when officers choose whether or not to enforce the law, they do so either on the basis of information which has been gathered prior to arrest, possibly with the aid of 'neutral' technology, or on the basis of an assessment founded less on common sense than on an understanding of the diagnostic practices of the social services. The likelihood that a suspect will be abused is reduced; the police retain parity with their fellow professionals.

Finally, the established militaristic style of command changed quite dramatically to one of 'management'. Discipline remained paramount but was to be maintained more by persuasion, consultation and encouragement than by enforcing blind obedience to authoritative commands. A profession manages itself, mobilizing all the skills of motivation, task determination, delegation and so on that it can muster. One of the Assistant Commissioners of the Metropolitan Police, writing about 'man management' during the 1960s, made this point:

> Studies have shown that a democratically led group may become highly disciplined and efficient. Under democracy, the will of the group dominates and social pressure will force individuals into line. In other words, the discipline is from within the group, that is to say, self-discipline. Such self-discipline is easier to maintain than a forced discipline under autocratic rule where the force must be wielded from outside. (Mahir, 1966, p. 823)

Importantly, these features of 'managerialism' were first fostered among the supervisory ranks. Policy was to be fed down the hierarchy to the officer on the street; a well-qualified body of police managers would gradually remould the attitudes and practices of the lower ranks. The process was to be one of gradual, disciplined education rather than militaristic prescription.

All of these emphases can be identified in unit beat policing and, indeed, in more recent innovations like community policing. Unit beat policing involves specialist home beat or community constables, whose day-to-day patrol work promotes public confidence. These officers are also responsible for the collection of evidence on known and suspected criminals; they are, as the Home Office report *Police Manpower, Equipment and Efficiency* put it, the 'eyes and ears' of the car patrol drivers and liaison detectives (Home Office, 1967). As such, the home beat officer assists the business of gathering information for the collated bank of data on local patterns of crime and criminals used to encourage the collection of evidence before arrest.

At Hilton during each shift of eight hours Panda cars patrol the subdivision, each in contact with the police station via the personal and force radio system. Here technology and some specialization combine to speed the reaction of Hilton's PCs to calls for assistance from the public. Recommending the unit beat method, the report suggested:

> we should expect to elevate the status of the beat constable in a way that would bring out the best qualities of a policeman – self-discipline, personal initiative and discretion – and challenge his intelligence, as well as his maturity and common sense, from the outset. (ibid., p. 118)

By implication, all patrolling officers should experience a sense of involvement in their work, especially when listening to the activity of policing on their radios. Of beat patrolling under existing systems this comment was made:

> There are probably many young policemen who find it difficult to derive much interest or satisfaction from working their beats in the traditional manner in urban areas. The work might be more readily tolerated if the conditions of service provided some measure of atonement for the boredom, but they do not. (ibid., p. 116)

The working party then went on to suggest that more recruits, not least those with solid educational qualifications, might be attracted to the force by the involvement and responsibility offered by unit beat policing. Sergeants are of particular importance as 'front-line' supervisors; indeed, the working party argued that they should receive considerable training in managerial techniques.

The implications of managerial professionalism for the higher and intermediate ranks are fairly clear. Professionalization is concerned with the internal standards of policing, the values of public service and proper public accountability. However, whether by design or as an unintended consequence, professionalization has led the police away from public control and influence – minimal as that has always been – towards an increasingly politicized role. This reclaiming of police status and authority under the banner of professionalism has, until very recently, tended to free chief officers from the constraints of their police authority (Brogden, 1977, 1982), has permitted the formulation and implementation of policies with little or no public consultation and has led to the intervention of the police in public and explicitly political debate and to the cultivation of a powerful collective police view in negotiations with the Home Office (Alderson, 1982; Hall, 1980). The notion of the police as a professional body is therefore both symbolic and instrumental – symbolic in that the freedom assured by the idea of professionalism has enhanced their status and authority, instrumental in that it has also permitted all manner of policies to be implemented in the name of this symbolic competence. One of the defining characteristics of a profession is precisely that it is a body which can, and does, claim significant autonomy in the ordering of its own affairs (Becker, 1970; Johnson, 1982).

Although it is manifest primarily in managerial policies, professional policing is also supposed to impinge upon the manner in which the rank and file should work. If we begin from Maureen Cain's (1973) description of urban policing prior to the professionalization of the service, it is possible to anticipate a number of implications for the day-to-day policing of Hilton.

First, the stress on action, on 'search, chase and capture', fight and scuffle and techniques which span the boundary of legality, should diminish. Managerial professionalism recognizes the importance of peacekeeping. In short, professionalism strikes a blow for a sensitive and conciliatory style of police work.

Secondly, importance should be placed upon both the strengthening of existing relationships between the police and the community policed and the creation of new ones. The 'easing' which Cain identified could provide a basis for sustaining these relations. Indeed, the emphasis placed by professional policing on the individual responsibility of each officer promotes the integration of crime-fighting and peacekeeping work within a broad framework of sensitivity to the population policed.

Thirdly, appreciation of the rule of law and closer co-operation with statutory agencies implies a less secretive and interdependent work group than that which Maureen Cain identified. Certainly, the extra-legal techniques of policing, especially those relevant to the questioning and charging processes within the station, should not be regarded as viable.

Fourthly, if peacekeeping and crime work are recognized as necessary components of the policeman's work load, the exclusive focus on crime which Cain identified should be balanced by an appreciation of the breadth of the role of the police. Arrest and clear-up rates need not be the primary indicators of effective policing.

Finally, the sense of policing a population which is ignorant of the demands of police work should be replaced by some appreciation of human diversity within the local population; competing demands for police service should be regarded as means by which to gain public co-operation and consent.

One feature of policing at Hilton, perhaps the most striking, is the continuing dominance of the occupational values and associated strategies of action which Cain (1973) documented prior to the professionalization of the service and the introduction of unit beat policing. Indeed, it seems that when the perspective of the lower ranks – their 'practical professionalism' – is moulded within this system of patrol, the occupational culture is enhanced rather than dulled. Policy is interpreted to accord with the ideas of the lower ranks. The assumption that policy moves straightforwardly down the hierarchy of police managers to the lower ranks is spurious. The technology of cars and radios has been exploited to sustain and heighten the experience of policing as action and fun. In particular, radio communication has promoted a stronger interdependency between the lower ranks than has previously been identified. The team character of policing bolsters the protection of the lower ranks' world. Police cars provide an official means of 'easing', reducing contact with the public. 'Easing' has been transformed into time spent in vehicles or at the station waiting for real police work – action – to occur.

Within the station the staff manages space and time, and the work group itself is organized to ensure the continuing power of the occupational culture. Claiming privacy in the charge room and cell areas, officers are able to work largely as they think appropriate; many of their practices are somewhat informal when assessed by legal criteria. At the time of research little evidence of the creation of trust or communication between the police and the population policed from Hilton is evident. When the manner in which the PCs perceive the population is considered, it seems that the dominant typifications are those moulded by officers' resistance to constraints designed to limit police action. Finally, the specialization found in professional policing has tended to stress rather than to modify the importance of crime work. This aspect of policing, which appeals to the officers' constant search for action, remains the primary measure of effectiveness.

In short, the occupational culture of urban policing as it is identified at Hilton is sustained by the lower ranks, despite the introduction of policies associated with professional policing. More than this, many of the features of police work identified by Cain (1973) before the 'professional era' appear to have survived intact and have certainly not been weakened by professional policies.

The development of professional policing has therefore entailed greater freedom for all ranks of the force. Chief and senior officers articulate and implement, frequently in a political context, policies appropriate to managerial professionalism which, in fact, often free them from significant public constraint. The old views and practices of the rank and file, though very often in opposition to the supposed intentions of managerial policy, persist under the powerful symbolic canopy of professionalism. Law and policy is remoulded within the crucible of the occupational culture.

Contemporary debate about the police

The point of detailing the process of police professionalization and its adaptation, if not neutralization, in unit beat policing is not of purely historical interest. Current attempts to change policing have to come to terms with the context within which that change is effected. If, as seems to be the case, the policing of Hilton is not wholly unlike that of other metropolitan centres, the resistance of lower ranks may be more of a stumbling block to reform than is presently appreciated (Brown, 1982; Chatterton, 1975a and b; Home Office, 1981; Punch, 1979b; Southgate, 1982).

There is a tendency among senior officers to regard the days of

'Panda policing' as an error which cannot be repeated if less emphasis is placed on motorized systems of patrol. The new era of community policing apparently ushers in a return to the traditional form of British policing by consent, in which contact between the beat policeman and the public is at a premium (Alderson, 1979). Yet it is hardly ever recalled that one aspect of unit beat policing and professionalization was precisely to enhance the responsiveness and sensitivity of the police to the public; for example, one intention of unit beat policing was 'to elevate the status of the beat constable in a way that would bring out the best qualities of a policeman – self-discipline, personal initiative and discretion – and challenge his intelligence, as well as his maturity and common sense, from the outset' (Home Office, 1967, p. 118).

Unit beat policing was not the aberration it is now often made out to be. The demands that it made on a meagre pool of manpower may have been too great, resulting in an over-emphasis on Panda patrol; sergeants and inspectors may have been inadequately prepared for their new managerial role. These and other factors have to be taken into account. However, the important point is quite simply that lower ranks were able to subvert the new system of patrol and to modify it so that their understanding of policing remained dominant.

Neither should we think that the working style of the lower ranks found in unit beat policing is novel. The policing of Hilton is clearly related to the 'good old days' of foot patrol amply documented by Cain (1973) and Chatterton (1979), which were more similar to unit beat policing than to a romantic community policing. If the Chief Constables who echo the words of Mr Barry Pain, at one time Chief Constable of Kent and presently Commandant of the Police Staff College – 'I've been employing community policing for years' (Judge, 1981) – have in mind a radically different approach from that evidenced here, they address a void. What has been documented at Hilton will not be easily redirected under any new system of patrol.

There is no doubt that it is preferable to increase contact between patrolling officers and members of the public. The various blends of community policing are not being rejected – indeed, they will be advocated. However, the initial and abiding point is that it is the lower ranks, about whose importance so much is said, who have the power to sabotage policy if it does not reflect their values. In the inner city there is a marked tension between the police reformers and the rank and file. And this is not just a matter of the lower ranks fulfilling their own desires; the organizational setting in which the bulk of police work is carried out actually facilitates the dominance of their occupational culture.

Much police work is done in private settings – in a room of a house, in a shop, an office or a car. Someone calls for assistance, and an officer arrives to make decisions in a context of very low visibility (Bottomley, 1973, p. 37). Since such private settings are often provided by members of the public who summon officers, and since each officer is expected to display individual competence, supervision becomes very difficult. It is simply not possible for a police manager to attend every incident that has prompted a member of the public to ask for the services of an officer; neither do PCs expect a sergeant to intervene in their adjudication of say, a family dispute. Further, we allow officers a wide discretion in the use of law, which tends to increase the power of the operational officer and to discourage the intervention of a supervisor with ideas that are rather different from those of his subordinates (ibid.).

The low visibility of officers and the discretionary and largely trusting nature of police work render the managerial staff largely dependent upon their subordinates for information about what is happening at Hilton (or anywhere else). Unless officers choose to make arrests, stop suspicious people, report disturbances and traffic offences, it is very difficult for police managers to know what is happening in their subdivision or, indeed, to feel confident that anything at all is being accomplished. They therefore tend to rely on the most readily accessible indicator, the figures for crimes reported and arrests made, which can be utterly misleading, as is a good deal of the other information imparted by patrolling officers. A number of researchers have argued that constables' reports of incidents are usually retrospective accounts (Lyman and Scott, 1967), couched in terms that meet the formal requirements of force rules, rather than representations of what has actually happened (Chatterton, 1979). A patrolling officer wants to protect himself from the charge – and there are disciplinary charges for just about everything – that he did nothing or the wrong thing. He constructs the appropriate account. This asymmetrical relationship between senior and junior police officers enhances the power of the lower ranks and makes the assessment of the effectiveness of police work an exceedingly complex task.

This imbalance between the supervisory and lower ranks' access to accurate information is further compounded by the ambiguity and uncertainty of many incidents (Chatterton, 1981). Officers arrive at troublesome scenes where competing accounts of events are presented, often in inarticulate, angry and garbled tones; more or less information is offered as a tentative inquiry proceeds; time presses. Such settings plunge the policeman into the difficult business of unravelling what seems to have occurred, what might be expected of him and what he might do. No matter how clearly a law may be framed, its application is generally as uncertain as the truth of an incident itself; there are no clear guides for settling conflict. Ambiguity and uncertainty cannot be allowed to persist, so recourse is made to the expedients of the occupational culture, which mediate legal and force directions. When an officer knows that his work may be reviewed by his supervisors after an incident, and that their review will take account of a vast number of procedural rules which can invoke criticism and more should they find evidence of mishandling, a certain caution in the reporting of incidents becomes a part of routine police work. Hence the ambiguity and uncertainty of policing will not disappear; we will always have to extend a measure of trust to our police.

Within this organizational framework policing is further influenced by a British social structure typified by persistent social inequality (Hall *et al.*, 1978). When, for example, the map of Hilton's population is analysed, it is clear that the attention paid by officers to blacks, and their attitude towards them, are not unrelated to the disadvantaged position of blacks in our society; the general clamour to control the territory of Hilton has a differential impact upon groups who are unable to find sanctuary in their own private spaces, which the police do not enter; the less well educated, and therefore the less articulate, are less able to complain about police behaviour (and the solicitors who represent them are seen as a threat to police autonomy). This is not to argue that policing reflects directly the primacy of ruling classes or elites – it vies with and yields to the pressure of class and power – but to recognize further limitations on police action (Brogden, 1982; Hall *et al.*, 1978).

These, then, represent some organizational and societal constraints on policing, which set the scene for reform.

The future

Current debate about policing tends to neglect the conditions under which patrolling officers actually work. The managerial model, in which policy flows fairly freely down the organization from rank to rank, still tends to dominate the ideas of sociologists and politicians (Dean, 1982; GLC, 1982; Taylor, 1981, pp. 146–64). The critical point of policy implementation, when an officer brings the resources of the occupational culture to bear on an incident, remains largely untouched.

The key contemporary issue is the public accountability of the police, the question of whether they should retain their present powers, backed and informed by a wider system of statutory liaison (Alderson, 1981; Dean, 1982; GLC, 1982; Holdaway, 1981). Further discussion concerns the manner in which complaints against the police should be investigated and adjudicated. Some argue for a partially independent element in the investigation procedure; others want a wholly independent system of inquiry. Yet others ask for better police training, a closer liaison between the police and the social services, the posting of more officers to foot patrol.

There can be no doubt of the pressing need for the reform of police authorities. My own view is that their present membership of councillors and magistrates should be reconstituted – broadened but not enlarged – to replace the magistracy with the representatives of various interests. The Metropolitan Police should most certainly come under more local control. (The new Manpower Service Boards may devise a pattern for how various interests can be brought together to fulfil an important monitoring function.) However, police authorities should be able to go further than the business of monitoring police policy. With a reconstituted membership somewhat freed from party political preferences and control but, of course, still dealing with political issues (for that is what issues of policing are), the authorities should be granted powers rather different from those they presently hold. Chief Constables should be required to consider policy reforms which do not interfere with their day-to-day operational decision-making but are concerned with the broad themes of police policy. There should, as Jack Straw, MP, proposed in his Police Authorities Bill, be a statutory period during which a Chief Constable can consider contentious and disputed proposals and ultimately appeal to the Home Secretary. Such police issues and other matters should be informed by discussion in local liaison groups, which would support the work of the police authority and provide a more personal link between divisional police commanders and the residents of a local area. Each police authority should publish an annual report detailing how the system of liaison is operating and how their own duties are being fulfilled (Cain, 1977).

Some would argue that these reforms are cumbersome and unnecessary, that all we require is a local liaison scheme to supplement the existing police authorities (Home Office, 1981). However, the professionalization and politicization of the police during recent years, together with the welcome innovation of community policing, which draws senior officers increasingly into debate about the allocation of local government financial and other resources, have to be checked and balanced by changes of the type I have outlined.* As this book is written, proposals for reform are before Parliament; debate will continue.

Much as change is required at this high-ranking level of the police organization, most current proposals for improving the accountability of the police focus only on influencing the policy-making of senior ranks and are therefore less than satisfactory. It is assumed that a change in general policy will be implemented largely by intermediate and lower-ranked officers in their routine work. Accountability here means taking into consideration a public view *before* decisions are made within the police. But suppose for a moment that it is possible to bring influence to bear upon the Chief Officer of Hilton's force through some new system of public liaison. How would new policies fare in the context of the occupational culture? Similarly, let us suppose that a wholly independent element were introduced into the complaints procedure. Would that really make major inroads into the routine policing of Hilton? Would new training schemes or simply putting more officers on beat patrol change a great deal?

* John Alderson's candidature for Parliament may well represent the logic of his policies of community policing in Devon and Cornwall.

Important and necessary as these and other proposed innovations are, they remain less than adequate because they all attempt to bring a greater measure of public accountability into play *before* (in the case of police authorities) or *after* (in the case of the investigation of complaints against the police) the police act. Yet routine police work in urban areas involves considerable discretion; policy is moulded by the lower ranks to conform with the occupational culture. Unless we have some idea about how policy is filtered through the occupational culture and refracted in one direction or another, little real accountability can be assured. The emphasis therefore has to be as much on accountability *at the time* that police work is carried out as on accountability before and after the police act (Holdaway, 1982b). This means that reform should be directed to maximizing the visibility of routine policing as it takes place, which is clearly an extremely difficult business.

Although the questioning and charging of suspects at the police station are not the dominant aspects of an officer's work (McBarnet, 1981b; Royal Commission, 1980), they do have a central place in the occupational culture. Their broader, symbolic focus as a touchstone of the character of policing in Britain and an indicator of the humanity of the political state should not be underestimated. If real improvements can be made in this area, public confidence may well increase and promote a broader appreciation of the problems of policing.

In its recent report the Royal Commission on Criminal Procedure (1981) argues that three principal standards have to govern the rules concerning the procedures of questioning and charging persons held in custody. Are they fair? Are they open? Are they workable? 'We prefer, then, rules whose breach can be clearly demonstrated both at the time and ex-post facto' (ibid., p. 109). Clearly, this proposal comes close to an attempt to open up the questioning and charging process to public view and therefore to make some impression upon the occupational culture. However, when it comes to its more specific proposals, the Commission adopts what it calls 'the necessity principle' (ibid., pp. 44–6): when the police decide to arrest a person, refuse bail, refuse or grant access to a solictor – when they decide to withhold any legal provision from a suspect – they must demonstrate the reasons for their action at the time. The decision to withhold legal provision will rest not necessarily with the officers making the arrest but with senior supervisory staff on duty at the relevant time and, though within a longer-term perspective, by one of Her Majesty's Inspectors of Constabulary during his annual force inspection. Every decision to withhold a legal provision should be recorded by what the Home Office Consultative Document *Rules Governing the Treatment and Questioning of Persons in Police Custody* calls a police 'custody officer', who also has the task of explaining procedural decisions to persons detained at the station.

This interpretation of 'openness' was developed by the Commission from the written and oral evidence placed before it, some specially commissioned research and summaries of previous published work on the criminal justice system (Royal Commission, 1981, p. 221). However, despite some promptings, it did not pay too much attention to one of the findings of sociological research into the police, perhaps the dominant one: in the course of routine work, and especially within the confines of the police station, lower ranks are able to reorient policy directives so that they accord with their own definition and practice of police work. Further, immediate supervisory officers can easily be drawn into and form part of a somewhat closed and secretive work group, which is highly interdependent and difficult to penetrate. Nevertheless, the Commission suggests: 'The duty to see that these rules are obeyed should rest in the first instance where it does now, with the police service (ibid., p. 111).

Not all forces follow the same procedure for questioning and charging as that used by Hilton's force. Nevertheless, if the Commission had given more consideration to the practical distinction between law-in-the-books and law-in-use it would have given much more weight to the introduction of some form of duty solicitor scheme under which advice would be available to a suspect at the time of initial questioning; to introducing an exclusion rule;* to the full tape-recording and, possibly, limited video-recording of interviews involving a statement of confes-

---

* In *New Society*, 6 January 1983, Martin Kettle reports on some research by Superintendent Tony Butler of the West Midlands Police into British and American policemen's view of the exclusion rule. Kettle summarizes: 'The message to policy-makers is clear: exclusionary rules may protect suspects after the event, but they seem to do little to control police action before it' (p. 18).

sion;* to, as Lord Scarman recommended, the granting to magistrates and the members of police authorities freedom of access at any time to persons detained and to the charge room and cell areas, without right of police objection. No doubt the Commissioners would argue that a number of these proposals are unworkable (which tends to mean too expensive) or unfair. The major point is that if the Commission's stated principle of openness finds its way into legislation as it stands, it is unlikely to be translated into practice by officers in their day-to-day work. Time will reveal the truth of this argument.

Many criticisms and alternative proposals for reform tend to be viewed negatively by the police. There is certainly an appreciation of the contemporary issues of policing amongst many Chief Constables; and senior staff. We can be less than certain about the intermediate ranks and the rank and file (Brown, 1982). Unless a balancing series of what the police come to regard as positive rewards can attract the lower ranks to accept reform, and these are seen as incentives by supervisory staff, we risk creating an even more beleaguered and defensive British force than exists at the moment.

One of Lord Scarman's recommendations (Home Office, 1981, p. 129) hints that chief officers should monitor official statistics of crime more carefully. The fallacies of formal rates as measures of actual criminal behaviour and the impact of police policy are well documented (for example, see Bottomley and Coleman, 1981). However, remembering that in Hilton's force these figures remain virtually the sole criterion for judging the performance of policing, greater emphasis now has to be placed on the formulation of a more comprehensive measure of police effectiveness (Hough, 1980a and b; Manning, 1977, pp. 347–53). This measure has to take realistic account of the limitations of police as preventers and detectors of crime, of the fact that fear of crime among the public can often be ill-matched to actual and reported levels of criminal activity (Morris and Heal, 1981, p. 52) and that a great deal of police work is only loosely related to crime, requiring the effective management of conflict between persons in dispute, often demanding a precarious balance of

---

* *The Times*, 29 November 1982, reported that the Home Office experiments concerned with the tape-recording of interviews had run into trouble. Officers apparently explained how they 'often adopt the tactic of engaging in "preliminary" interviews elsewhere'.

police patience and firmness (Punch, 1979a). Any new measure of effectiveness which may be pressed upon the Home Office and Chief Constables more by a lack of financial resources to increase manpower in the wake of apparently rising crime than by any of principle should take this broad mandate into account. Full consultation on its formulation would have to take place with police authorities and local liaison groups. They would have to accept that their pressure on police to cut overall crime rates has to be tempered, that they are interested in the quality as well as the quantity of police work in both the criminal and the peacekeeping areas.

The difficulties of an exercise like this should not be underestimated; it could not be accomplished overnight. Nevertheless, once work on a new measure has begun and it is formulated, fewer unrealistic expectations may be placed upon police; patrol strategies which do seem to have some impact on some types of crime and levels of public safety can be employed more confidently; peacekeeping can be recognized as a key element of routine police work. In the longer term, public expectations of what the police can and cannot accomplish might be more truthful and sensible; chief officers might be somewhat freed from juggling with the pressures of unrealistic public demands and therefore more able to tackle those competing claims for police service which actually have some relevance to the impact of police in society, rather than police and public folklore. Much here depends on the capacity of police authorities and liaison groups – of all of us – to create an atmosphere in which the police are able to discuss the limitations of their policies without fear of ridicule. Just as the police have to break out of their protective shell, so we have to accept that the goodness of policing cannot be more fully tapped unless we give up being unrealistic about policing.

In his research of a major British force Mervyn Jones, himself a police officer, found that although his Chief Constable articulated his belief in the importance of the beat constable as the foundation of his force's work, little real incentive was actually given to keep officers on the beat and little notice was taken of their preventive work (Jones, 1980, pp. 92–111). The typical young probationer wanted to be promoted or to join a specialist department as soon as possible; force policy encouraged as much. Those constables who had made a positive decision to

[margin handwritten note: → Related to Public Compromise]

remain on the beat were viewed suspiciously as 'uniform carriers'; they were thought to lack the motivation of their promotion-conscious peers. Beat work was demeaned. This is an imbalance that probably exists in many forces; it has to be redressed and Jones's model of research could well be refined to a formal check-list used by police authorities to monitor whether or not sufficient attention is being paid to its constables.

New criteria for police effectiveness are of relevance here. When Jones looked at the commendations awarded to officers for good work, crime control and law enforcement formed the rationale for reward; preventive policing and peacekeeping was seldom recognized. And how could it be recognized as integral to the work of the organization when it forms no real part of the police criteria of effectiveness? A reconstituted measure might well begin to break into managerial policy and practice which encouraged, and at times rewarded, this type of work. Beat work would be enhanced, the breadth of police work given proper recognition.

Similar attention has to be given to lower ranking supervisors. The stress on 'managerialism', which formed part of the professionalization of the British police and the system of unit beat policing has, at one and the same time, given sergeants an extremely demanding role. They are expected to work more closely with their constables and employ management techniques for which they have little or no training. As Michael Chatterton noticed in his (1981) research of an urban force using the system of unit beat policing, it was the PCs who ultimately decided whether a sergeant would get involved in their work. A great deal has to be done to prepare and support sergeants – and inspectors too – in their work developing their advisory role with PCs, creating a setting in which their proximity and involvement in the police team is recognized as a positive means of developing much more effective supervision.

The balance of policies – crime and public order, generalist and specialist, peacekeeping and law enforcement – within individual constabularies is in need of more careful monitoring. Evidence to support this point is fairly scanty, but it does seem that many Chief Constables have articulated their response to pressure for reform by improving their public relations policies, putting more men on beat patrol, developing school visiting programmes and so on. However, as much as they have done this, they have also ploughed thousand upon thousands of pounds into technology for computerized systems of 'command and control', designed to speed up response time to a call from a member of the public for police assistance. (Hough, 1980a and b) Equal effort has been put into the creation of 'instant response squads' to deal with public disorder; into special patrol or similar groups; firearms training and, ironically, over-specialized community involvement, race relations and other similar departments (Bunyan and Kettle, 1980). Some of these innovations may be necessary, reflecting the complex demands made of police. However, the point is that one gets the feeling that they are never really weighed within the balance of policies any one force employs in the fulfilment of its work. For example, the use of computers for information storage and for 'command and control' could well be decided by police fashions and one-upmanship rather than any other criteria of need (Hough, 1980a and b). At the moment the burden of deciding upon how policies relate to each other rests with the chief officer; this is a burden better shared with a wider constituency of interest. Further, remembering what we know of the occupational culture, we can only wonder about the relative weight PCs give to what they regard as the 'soft' and 'hard' policies of their chief officers.

These types of issue, involving the more public discussion of problems which the police face, could help to create a societal context where the capacity of police to control crime and disorder and respond to public demands is faced more honestly – not least because there is much to be gained by the police themselves. Again, a great deal depends upon our police feeling that they are in a situation where they are able to articulate their limitations to police authorities and local liaison groups without retreating into the haven of professionalism. Equally, much depends on the members of these bodies being sufficiently sensitive to permit the police to admit their weakness; there is a double-edged character to this task.

But it is always necessary to return to the implementers of policy – the lower ranks – as to those who formulate it. A good deal of police work on the streets is uninviting and unattractive; walking streets on a wet and cold day is simply uncomfortably tough; dealing with other people's bickerings a ready motivator for cynicism; helping the victims of crime and disorder a temptation to bitterness; bandaging physical and psychic wounds can be plain sick-making. Yet these are other constants of the business of policing, which at the moment cannot be fully appreciated because they are subsumed within an occupational culture that diverts attention to other matters. Further, the frequently sung romantic praises of the police constantly beg the reminder that we refer to a powerful institution in our society where social inequality of material circumstance tends to weigh them against the less powerful. That, as Bittner (1970, p. 46) has put it, the central defining characteristic of police is their 'capacity to use situationally justified force'. Public accountability is therefore of the essence of police in a democratic society; public participation in police policymaking has to tackle accountability before, after and, so far as is possible, as the police act.

These, then, are the central policy issues arising from this study of policing at Hilton. The tightly bound culture of the lower ranks has to be broken into; the virtual sanctity of police policy has to be demystified, not just to denounce but also to check power and to gain a wider appreciation of the possibilities and limitations of policing. Whatever reforms might be effected, more attention has to be paid to the lower ranks as they work from day to day. The occupational culture remains the final testing ground of sociological analysis and policy intervention.

References

Alderson, J. (1981), *Submission to Scarman: The Case for Community Policing,* London: Concern

Alderson, J. C. (1973), 'The principles and practice of the British police', in J. C. Alderson and P. J. Stead (eds.), *The Police We Deserve,* London: Wolfe

Alderson, J. (1979), *Policing Freedom: A Commentary on the Dilemmas of Policing in Western Democracies,* Plymouth: Macdonald and Evans

Alderson, J. 1982: 'Policing in the eighties: interview with Chief Constable John Alderson', *Marxism Today,* April, pp.8–14

Ardrey, R. (1966), *The Territorial Imperative,* New York: Atheneum

Ball, D. (1973), *Microecology: Social Situations and Intimate Space,* Chicago: Bobbs-Merrill

Banton, M. (1964), *The Policeman in the Community,* London: Tavistock

Bayley, D. H., and Mendelsohn, H. (1968), *Minorities and the Police: Confrontation in America,* New York: Free Press

Becker, H. S. (1970), *Sociological Work,* London: Allen Lane

Berger, P. L., and Luckman, T. (1967), *The Social Construction of Reality,* London: Allen Lane

Bettelheim, B. (1943), 'Individual and mass behaviour in extreme situations', *J. Abnormal & Soc. Psychol.,* 38, pp. 417–52.

Bittner, E. (1965), 'The concept of organisation', *Social Res.,* 32 (Winter), pp. 239–55

Bittner, E. (1967), 'The police on Skid-Row: a study of peace keeping', *Amer. Sociol. Rev.,* 32 (5), pp. 699–715

Bittner, E. (1970), *The Functions of the Police in Modern Society,* Washington: National Institute of Mental Health

Bottomley, A. K. (1973) *Decisions in the Penal Process*, London: Martin Robertson

Bottomley, A. K., and Coleman, C. A. (1981), *Understanding Crime Rates: Police and Public Roles in the Production of Official Statistics*, Farnborough: Gower

British Sociological Association (1973), *Statement of Ethical Principles and their Application to Sociological Research*

Brogden, M. (1977), 'A police authority – the denial of conflict', *Sociol. Rev.*, 25 (2), pp. 325–49

Brogden, M. (1982), *The Police: Autonomy and Consent*, London: Academic Press

Brown, J. (1982), *Policing by Multi-Cultural Consent*, London: Bedford Square Press

Bunyan, T., and Kettle, M. (1980), 'The police force of the future is now here', *New Society*, 21 August, pp. 351–4

Cain, M. E. (1973), *Society and the Policeman's Role*, London: Routledge and Kegan Paul

Cain, M. (1977), 'An ironical departure: the dilemma of contemporary policing', in K. Jones *et al.* (eds.), *The Yearbook of Social Policy in Britain*, London: Routledge and Kegan Paul

Cain, M. (1979), 'Trends in the sociology of police work', *Internat. J. of the Sociol. of Law*, 7, pp. 143–67.

Carlen, P. (1976) *Magistrates' Justice*, London: Martin Robertson

Centre for Research on Criminal Justice (1975), *The Iron Fist and the Velvet Glove – An Analysis of the US Police*, Berkeley, California: Centre for Research on Criminal Justice

Chatterton, M. (1975a), *Images of Police Work and the Uses of Rules: Supervision and Patrolwork under the Fixed Points System*, paper presented at the Third Conference on the Sociology of the Police, Bristol

Chatterton, M. (1975b), 'Organisational relationships and processes in police work: a case study of urban policing', unpublished Ph.D. thesis, University of Manchester

Chatterton, M. R. (1979), 'The supervision of patrol work under the fixed points system', in S. Holdaway (ed.), *The British Police*, London: Edward Arnold

Chatterton, M. R. (1981), *Practical Coppers, Oarsmen and Administrators: Front-Line Supervisory Styles in Police Organizations*, paper presented to ISA Research Committee on the Sociology of Law, Oxford

Chibnall, S. (1977), *Law-and-Order News: An Analysis of Crime Reporting in the British Press*, London: Tavistock

Clarke, J., *et al.* (1974), 'The selection of evidence and the avoidance of racialism: a critique of the Parliamentary Select Committee on Race Relations and Immigration', *New Community*, 111 (3), pp. 172–92

Clarke, M. (1975), 'Survival, in the field: implications of personal experience in field work', *Theory and Society*, 2, pp. 95–123

Coser, R. L. (1959), 'Some social functions of laughter: a study of humor in a hospital setting', *Human Relations*, 12, pp. 171–81

Coser, R. L. (1960), 'Laughter among colleagues: a study of the social functions of humour among the staff of a mental hospital', *Psychiatry*, 23, pp. 81–95

Dean, M. (1982), 'The finger on the policeman's collar', *Political Quarterly*, 53, (2), pp. 153–64

Ditton, J. (1979), 'Baking time', *Sociological Review*, 27 (1), pp. 157–67

Douglas, M. (1975), *Implicit Meanings: Essays in Anthropology*, London: Routledge and Kegan Paul

Festinger, L., *et al.* (1956), *When Prophecy Fails*, Minneapolis: University of Minnesota Press

Fletcher, J. (1966), *Situation Ethics*, London: SCM Press

Glaser, B. G., and Strauss, A. L. (1967), 'Awareness contexts and social interaction', *Amer. Sociol. Rev.*, 29, pp. 669–79

GLC (1982), *Policing London*, London: Greater London Council

Goffman, E. (1969) *The Presentation of Self in Everyday Life*, Harmondsworth: Penguin

Goffman, E. (1971), *Relations in Public: Microstudies of the Public Order*, Harmondsworth: Penguin

Goffman, E. (1972), *Interaction Ritual: Essays on Face-to-Face Behaviour*, Harmondsworth: Penguin

Gold, R. L. (1958), 'Roles in sociological field observations', *Social Forces*, 36, pp. 217–33

Goldstein, J. (1960), 'Police discretion not to invoke the criminal process. Low visibility decisions in the administration of justice', *Yale Law Journal*, 69, pp. 543–94

Greenwood, P. W., Chaiken, J. M., and Petersilia, J. (1977), *The Criminal Investigation Process*, Lexington: D. C. Heath

Hall, S. (1980), *Drifting in a Law and Order Society*, London: Cobden Trust

Hall, S., Critcher, C., Jefferson, T., Clarke, J., and Roberts, B.

(1978). *Policing the Crisis: Mugging, the State, and Law and Order*, London: Macmillan

Hannerz, U. (1969), *Soulside: Inquiries into Ghetto Culture and Community*, New York and London: Columbia University Press

Holdaway, S. (1977), 'Changes in urban policing', *British Journal of Sociology*, 28 (2), pp. 119–37

Holdaway, S. (1978), 'The reality of police race relations: towards an effective community relations policy', *New Community*, 6 (3), pp. 258–67

Holdaway, S. (1980), 'The police station', *Urban Life*, 9 (1), pp. 79–100

Holdaway, S. (1981), *The Occupational Culture of Urban Policing: An Ethnographic Study*, Ph.D. thesis, University of Sheffield

Holdaway, S. (1982a), 'An inside job: a case study of covert research on the police', in M. Bulmer (ed.), *Social Research Ethics*, London: Macmillan

Holdaway, S. (1982b), 'Police accountability: a current issue', *Public Administration*, 60, Spring, pp. 84–9

Homan, R. (1980), 'The ethics of covert research: Homan defends his methods', *Network*, January, p. 4

Home Office (1963), *Sheffield Police Appeal Enquiry*, Cmnd 2176, London: HMSO

Home Office (1965), *Report of Enquiry by Mr A. E. James, QC*, Cmnd 2735, London: HMSO

Home Office (1967), *Police Manpower, Equipment and Efficiency*, London: HMSO

Home Office (1977), *Report of an Enquiry by Hon. Sir Henry Fisher into the Circumstances Leading to the Trial of Three Persons on Charges Arising out of the Death of Maxwell Confait and the Fire at 27 Dogett Road, London, SE6*, London: HMSO

Home Office (1981), *The Brixton Disorders 10–12 April 1981. Report of an Enquiry by the Rt. Hon. The Lord Scarman, OBE*, London: HMSO

Horton, J. (1967), 'Time and cool people', *Transaction*, 7, pp. 5–12

Hough, J. M. (1980a) *Uniformed Police Work and Management Technology*, Research Unit Paper 1, London: Home Office

Hough, M. (1980b), 'Managing with Less Technology', *Brit. Jrn. Crim.*, 20 (4), pp. 344–57

Hughes, E. C. (1953), *Men and their Work*, New York: Free Press

Institute of Race Relations (1979), *Police against Black People: Evidence Submitted to the Royal Commission on Criminal Procedure,* Race and Class Pamphlet 6, London: Institute of Race Relations

James, D. (1979), 'Police–black relations: the professional solution', in S. Holdaway (ed.), *The British Police*, London: Edward Arnold

Johnson, T. (1972), *Professions and Power*, London: Macmillan

Jones, J. M. (1980), *Organizational Aspects of Police Behaviour*, Westmead: Gower

Judge, T. (1981), 'Alderson's Law', *Police*, 14 (2), p. 8

La Favre, W. R. (1965), 'The police and non-enforcement of the law', *Wisconsin Law Rev.*, 179, pp. 104–37

Lambert, J. 1970 *Crime, Police and Race Relations: A Study in Birmingham,* London: OUP for Institute of Race Relations

Lefkowitz, J. (1975), 'Psychological attributes of policemen', *J. Social Issues*, 31 (1), pp. 5–26

Loftland, J. (1961), 'Comment on initial interactions with newcomers in AA', *Social Problems*, 8, pp. 365–7

Lyman, S., and Scott, M. (1967), 'Territoriality: a neglected sociological dimension', *Social Problems*, 15 (2), pp. 236–49

Lyman, S., and Scott, M. (1970), 'Accounts, deviance and social order', in Jack Douglas (ed.), *Deviance and Respectability*, New York: Basic Books

McBarnet, D. (1981a), *Convictions: Law, the State and the Construction of Justice*, London, Macmillan

McBarnet, D. (1981b), 'The Royal Commission and the Judges' Rules', *Brit. J. Law and Society*, 8 (1), pp. 109–17

McConville, M., and Baldwin, J. (1982), 'The role of interrogation in crime discovery and conviction', *Brit. J. Criminol.*, 22 (1), pp. 165–75

Mahir, T. E. (1966), 'Managing people', *Police J.*, August, pp. 1–24

Manning, P. (1972), 'Observing the police', in Jack Douglas (ed.), *Research on Deviance*, New York: Random House

Manning, P. K. (1977), *Police Work: The Social Organization of Policing*, Cambridge, Mass., and London: MIT Press

Manning, P. K. (1978), 'Lying, secrecy and social control', in P. K. Manning and J. Van Maanen (eds.): *Policing: A View from the Street*, Santa Monica: Goodyear

Manning, P. K. (1979), 'The social control of police work', in S. Holdaway (ed.), *The British Police*, London: Edward Arnold

Manning, P. K. (1980), *The Narcs' Game: Organizational and Informational Limits on Drug Law Enforcement*, Cambridge, Mass., and London: MIT Press

Manning, P. K., and Van Maanen, J. (eds.) (1978), *Policing: A View from the Street*, Santa Monica: Goodyear

Mark, R. (1977), *Policing a Perplexed Society*, London: George Allen and Unwin

Matza, D. (1964), *Delinquency and Drift*, New York: Wiley

Mechanic, D. (1962), 'Sources of power of lower participants in complex organizations', *Admin. Sci. Q.*, 7, pp. 349–64

Moore, C., and Brown, J. (1981), *Community Versus Crime*, London: Bedford Square Press

Morris, P., and Heal, K. (1981), *Crime Control and the Police: A Review of Research*, Home Office Research Study No. 67, London: HMSO

Packer, H. L. (1964), 'Two models of the criminal process', *Univ. Pennsylvania Law Rev.*, 113, pp. 1–68.

Powis, D. (1977), *The Signs of Crime: a Field Manual for Police*, London: McGraw-Hill

Punch, M. (1979a), 'The secret social service', in Simon Holdaway (ed.), *The British Police*, London: Edward Arnold

Punch, M. (1979b), *Policing the Inner City: A Study of Amsterdam's Warmoesstraat*, London: Macmillan

Punch, M., and Naylor, T. (1973), 'The police: a social service', *New Society*, 24, pp. 358–61

Reed, M. S., Jr, Burnette, J., and Troiden, J. R. (1977), 'Wayward cops: the functions of deviance in groups reconsidered', *Social Problems*, 24 (5), pp. 565–75

Reiner, R. (1980), 'Fuzzy thoughts: the police and law-and-order politics', *Soc. Rev.*, 28 (2), pp. 377–413

Reiner, R. (1981), 'Black and blue: race and the police', *New Society*, 17 September, pp. 466–9

Reiss, A. (1965), 'Police brutality – answers to key questions', *Transaction*, 5 (8), pp. 10–19

Rock, P. (1973), *Deviant Behaviour*, London: Hutchinson

Rock, P. (1974), 'Conceptions of moral order', *Brit. J. Criminol.*, 14 (2), pp. 139–149

Rosenhan, D. L. (1973), 'On being sane in insane places', *Science*, 179, pp. 250–8

Roy, D. (1960), 'Banana time: job satisfaction and informal interaction', *Human Organization*, 18, pp. 156–68

Royal Commission on the Police (1962), *Final Report*, Cmnd 1728, London: HMSO

Royal Commission on Criminal Procedure (1980), *Police Interrogation: the Psychological Approach. A Case Study of Current Practice*, Research Studies Nos. 1 and 2, London: HMSO

Royal Commission on Criminal Procedure (1981), *Report*, Cmnd 8092, London: HMSO

Rubinstein, J. (1973), *City Police*, New York: Ballantine

Sacks, H. (1972), 'Notes on police assessment of moral character', in D. Sudnow (ed.), *Studies in Social Interaction*, New York: Free Press

Schutz, A. (1970a), *Reflections on the Problem of Relevance*, New Haven: Yale University Press

Schutz, A. (1970b) *On Phenomenology and Social Relations: Selected Writings*, ed. H. R. Wagner, Chicago: University of Chicago Press

Schutz, A. (1972), *The Phenomenology of the Social World*, trans. G. Walsh and F. Lehnert, London: Heinemann Educational Books

Schutz, A. (1974) *The Structures of the Life-World*, trans. T. Luckmann, R. M. Zaner, and H. T. Engelhardt, London: Heinemann Educational Books

Silverman, D. (1970), *The Theory of Organisations*, London: Heinemann Educational Books

Skolnick, J. H. (1966), *Justice without Trial: Law Enforcement in Democratic Society*, New York: John Wiley

Sommer, R. (1959), 'Studies in personal space', *Sociometry*, 22, September, pp. 247–60

Sommer, R. (1966), 'Man's proximate environment', *J. of Social Issues*, 22 (4), pp. 59–70

Southgate, P. (1982), *Police Probationer Training in Race Relations*, Home Office Research and Planning Unit Paper No. 8, London: HMSO

Stead, P. J. (1973), 'The idea of a police college', in J. C. Alderson and P. J. Stead (eds.), *The Police we Deserve*, London: Wolfe

Stevens, P., and Willis, C. F. (1979), *Race, Crime and Arrests*, Home Office Research Study No. 58, London: HMSO

Taylor, I. (1981), *Law and Order: Arguments for Socialism*, London: Macmillan

Taylor, I., Walton, P., and Young, J. (1973), *The New Criminology: For a Social Theory of Deviance,* London: Routledge and Kegan Paul

Taylor, I., Walton, P., and Young, J. (eds.) (1975), *Critical Criminology,* London: Routledge and Kegan Paul

Teahan, J. E. (1975), 'A longitudinal study of attitude shifts among black and white police officers', *J. Social Issues,* 31 (1), pp. 47–56

Thompson, E. P. (1967), 'Time, work discipline and industrial capitalism', *Past and Present,* 38, December, pp. 56–97

Toch, H. (1972) *Violent Men: An Inquiry into the Psychology of Violence,* Harmondsworth: Penguin

Toch, H., and Schulte, R. (1961), 'Readiness to perceive violence as a result of police training', *Brit. J. Psychol.,* 52 (4), pp. 389–93

Wallis, R. (1977), 'The moral career of a research project', in C. Bell and H. Newby (eds.), *Doing Sociological Research,* London: Allen and Unwin

Westley, W. (1970), *Violence and the Police: A Sociological Study of Law, Custom and Morality,* Cambridge, Mass.: MIT Press

Whyte, W. F. (1955), *Street Corner Society: The Social Structure of an Italian Slum,* London: University of Chicago Press

Wilson, T. P. (1971), 'Normative and interpretive paradigms in sociology', in J. Douglas (ed.), *Understanding Everyday Life,* London, Routledge and Kegan Paul, pp. 57–79

Young, J. (1970), 'The zookeepers of deviancy', *Catalyst,* 5, pp. 38–46

Zander, M. (1972), 'Access to a solicitor in the police station', *Criminal Law Review,* pp. 342–50

Zijderveld, A. C. (1968), 'Jokes and their relation to social reality', *Social Res.,* 35, pp. 286–311

Index of Subjects

Index of Names